ETHNOS

CROSS THE STREET.
REACH THE NATIONS.

Renod and Karen Bejjani

Copyright © 2026 Renod and Karen Bejjani

All rights reserved. No part of this publication may be reproduced in any form or by any electronic or mechanical means, including information storage and retrieval systems, without permission in writing by the publisher, except by a reviewer who may quote brief passages in a review. For information regarding permission, contact the publisher at info@iHOPEministries.org.

This book is available at special discounts when purchased in quantity for use as premiums, promotions, fundraisers, or for educational purposes. For inquiries and details, contact the authors at Karen@iHOPEministries.org.

Published by iHOPE Ministries
Dallas, Texas
iHOPEministries.org

Editing and Design by My Writers' Connection

Library of Congress Control Number: 2026900226
Paperback ISBN: 978-1-9516-1604-5
ebook ISBN: 978-1-951616-05-2

Scriptures marked AMP are taken from the AMPLIFIED BIBLE (AMP), Copyright © 1954, 1958, 1962, 1964, 1965, 1987 by the Lockman Foundation. Used by Permission. (www.Lockman.org)

Scriptures marked CSB are taken from the Christian Standard Bible®, Copyright © 2017 by Holman Bible Publishers. Used by permission. Christian Standard Bible® and CSB® are federally registered trademarks of Holman Bible Publishers.

Scriptures marked NASB are taken from the New American Standard Bible®, Copyright © 1960, 1971, 1977, 1995, 2020 by The Lockman Foundation. Used by permission. All rights reserved. Lockman.org

Scriptures marked NIV are taken from the Holy Bible, New International Version®, NIV®. Copyright © 1973, 1978, 1984, 2011 by Biblica, Inc.™ Used by permission of Zondervan. All rights reserved worldwide (www.Zondervan.com). The "NIV" and "New International Version" are trademarks registered in the United States Patent and Trademark Office by Biblica, Inc.™

Scriptures marked NKJV are taken from the New King James Version®. Copyright © 1982 by Thomas Nelson. Used by permission. All rights reserved.

Scriptures marked NLT are taken from the Holy Bible, New Living Translation, copyright ©1996, 2004, 2015 by Tyndale House Foundation. Used by permission of Tyndale House Publishers, Carol Stream, Illinois 60188. All rights reserved.

CONTENTS

About iHOPE Ministries v

ETHNOS Leader's Guide 1

The Foundation 11

Session 1: Understanding World Religions 19

Session 2: Start Spiritual Conversations 31

Session 3: The 5 Essentials + Love 45

Session 4: Look for a Person of Peace 57

Session 5: Pray Together, in Jesus' Name 67

Session 6: Share the Gospel, Early and Often 81

Session 7: Share the Bible 93

Appendix: Your Next Steps After ETHNOS 107

About the Authors 112

ABOUT iHOPE MINISTRIES

> **VISION**
> A movement of believers revealing Christ to the world.
>
> **MISSION**
> Ignite and equip believers to boldly reveal Christ across faiths.
>
> **TAGLINE**
> So the world may know.

iHOPE Ministries exists to grow a movement of everyday believers who confidently and compassionately reveal Christ across faith and cultural differences—right where God has placed them.

Founded in 2011 by Renod and Karen Bejjani, iHOPE Ministries was born out of a deep burden for people of other faiths and a conviction that ordinary Christians, empowered by the Holy Spirit, can play a vital role in God's global mission.

Through Scripture-rooted resources like this ETHNOS Course™ and The Blue Cord study, iHOPE Ministries helps believers move from fear to faith-filled action—engaging neighbors, coworkers, and classmates of other faiths with humility, wisdom, and hope. Hundreds of thousands of believers worldwide have been equipped through iHOPE resources to go from "I can't" to "I do" when it comes to sharing Jesus across faiths.

Learn more at iHOPEministries.org.

Welcome, Friend.

We're so glad you're here.

Your participation in ETHNOS™ is not an accident. We have been praying for you, and we know that God has uniquely positioned you—at this moment in history—for a purpose.

Our prayer for you is that you will be *inspired, equipped, and emboldened* to share Jesus across faiths in your everyday life—at work, at school, in your neighborhood, and beyond.

ETHNOS is more than a study. *It is a catalyst for transformation.*

As you journey through this course, you will:

- Grow in your understanding of God's heart for people of all nations
- Discover how God is already at work in the lives of people around you
- Learn simple, biblical practices for sharing Jesus across faiths in your daily life
- Move from hesitation to confident, Spirit-led obedience

Nine out of ten believers who complete ETHNOS find themselves doing more faith-sharing actions than they ever imagined possible. We believe the same will be true for you.

What Is ETHNOS?

The word *ethnos* comes from the Greek ἔθνος, meaning *nation, people, tribe, or people group*. Throughout Scripture, God's redemptive story consistently points toward his desire to bless and redeem *all nations*.

From the scattering at Babel (Genesis 11), to God's promise to Abraham that *all nations would be blessed through him* (Genesis 12:3), to the Great Commission (Matthew 28:19–20), and finally to the breathtaking vision of every nation worshiping before the throne (Revelation 7:9), God's heart for the *ethnos* has always been clear.

Today, the nations are no longer far away.

In God's providence, people from all over the world now live in our cities, attend our schools, work in our offices, and move into our neighborhoods. Many have never heard the gospel clearly—or experienced the love of Christ through a follower of Jesus.

ETHNOS was created for this moment.

What to Expect in This Course

ETHNOS is an **eight-session discipleship journey** designed to help you live as an authentic witness across faiths in your everyday life. Each session follows a consistent rhythm:

1. **Watch the video teaching**—Each session begins with a short video that introduces a core biblical concept.
2. **Engage real-life stories**—You'll read true stories from believers—and from people who came to faith from other religious backgrounds—showing what sharing Jesus could look like in everyday life.
3. **Reflect on Scripture**—Guided reflection will anchor each session in God's Word and invite the Holy Spirit to shape your thoughts and actions.
4. **Respond with an "I Will" statement**—Each session concludes with a simple, practical commitment—something you will put into practice before the next session.

Transformation happens when what you are learning moves from these pages into your real life.

How to Get the Most Out of ETHNOS

ETHNOS can be completed individually, but it is *most powerful when experienced in community*. With that in mind, we encourage you to invite a friend or two to do this study with you. As you embark on the study together, commit to the following:

- Complete one session per week.
- Share your reflections and "I Will" statements.
- Pray together and encourage one another.
- Celebrate the actions you take—whether the outcome feels successful or not.

Through this course, you will discover that you don't need to be an evangelist, a theologian, or a missionary to share Jesus with people from other nations and faith backgrounds. You simply need a willing heart, a few biblical tools, and a great love for Jesus.

God will take care of the rest.

> "For I am the Lord your God who takes hold of your right hand and says to you, 'Do not fear; I will help you.'"
>
> —ISAIAH 41:13, NIV

An Invitation

As you begin ETHNOS, ask God one simple question:

"Lord, what would you have me put into practice this week?"

Then take the next faithful step.

God is already at work—both in you and nonbelievers around you.

Before You Start the Course

Before beginning the first session, we invite you to take a short, anonymous survey. It will ask about your current thoughts, attitudes, and actions related to sharing your faith across faiths.

At the end of this course, you'll be invited to take the same short survey again—so you can clearly see how God has grown and stretched you through your ETHNOS Course journey.

To access the ETHNOS survey and all of the video teaching segments, go to EthnosCourse.org and register for an account. After you have created your account, you can log in to stream the video teaching any time.

TECH QUESTIONS?

We have answers! Just email IT@iHOPEministries.org.

ETHNOS LEADER'S GUIDE

IN THIS SECTION
- Tips for Group Facilitators
- How ETHNOS Is Designed to Work
- A Note to Youth Facilitators
- ETHNOS Session Flow
- Final Encouragement
- ETHNOS Facilitator Covenant

Tips for Group Facilitators

ETHNOS was designed for *everyday believers*—not experts—to help people follow Jesus across cultures and faith backgrounds. This coursebook is not a textbook to master or a script to perform. It is a tool for transformation, meant to be used in community, guided by the Holy Spirit, and lived out in everyday life.

If you are facilitating this course, your role is not to teach everything, explain everything, or prove anything. Your role is to create space—space for God's Word to speak, for people to reflect honestly, and for the Spirit to move hearts toward courageous obedience.

This section will help you understand how to

- use this coursebook wisely
- facilitate discussion effectively
- guide adults and youth (ages 12–15) through the ETHNOS course
- avoid common pitfalls that diminish transformation

> For expanded facilitator coaching, discipleship guidance, and troubleshooting tips, watch the **ETHNOS Facilitator Training Video** and download the companion guide available at EthnosCourse.org.

A Word of Encouragement to Facilitators

You do *not* need to be

- an expert in world religions
- experienced in cross-faith evangelism
- gifted in public speaking
- or confident in every answer

You *do* need to be

- willing to follow Jesus
- open to learning alongside others
- committed to drawing people out rather than impressing them
- faithful to the simple structure of this course

ETHNOS works not because facilitators know more—but because facilitators *make room*.

Your Role as an ETHNOS Facilitator

Think of yourself less as a teacher and more as a guide.

An effective ETHNOS facilitator:

- watches the video with the group,
- resists the urge to over-explain,
- keeps discussions focused and inclusive,
- protects time for Scripture and reflection,
- and continually points people back to Jesus—not to themselves.

The goal is not information.

The goal is *transformation*.

A Word Regarding Experienced or Knowledgeable Participants

In some groups, participants may have prior missions experience, deep cultural knowledge, or years of cross-faith engagement. While this experience is valuable, ETHNOS is not the place to showcase it.

As a facilitator, you can gently redirect participants when needed:

- "Let's hear from someone who hasn't shared yet."
- "That's helpful—how does this connect to what we just watched?"
- "Let's keep the focus on what God is inviting *us* to do."

The best facilitators draw people out by preventing any one person from dominating the discussion.

How ETHNOS Is Designed to Work

Each ETHNOS session contains more material than can be completed in a 60–90-minute group meeting. This is intentional.

In the group session, prioritize:

1. Watching the video together
2. Discussion
3. Scripture reflection
4. The "I Will" statement

Other coursebook content (stories, charts, explanations, examples) is designed for personal reading before or after each session, deeper reflection during the week, or reference as needed.

Do not try to cover everything in one meeting. Depth, not coverage, leads to transformation.

The Heart of ETHNOS: The 1-2-4-7 Discussion Method

Over years of real-world experience, we have found that *discussion—not lecture—is where transformation happens*. The 1-2-4-7 Discussion Method ensures that *every voice is heard*, not just the loudest or most experienced.

The 1-2-4-7 Method should be used for *all discussion questions* whenever possible.

1—Silent Processing (1 minute)

Participants silently reflect on the question. This time honors introverts, reduces pressure, and allows the Holy Spirit to speak.

2—Partner Sharing (2 minutes)

Participants turn to one person and share briefly. This lowers fear and builds confidence before group sharing.

4—Small Group Sharing (4 minutes)

Two pairs join together (groups of four) to share insights. During this time, patterns emerge, and people gain courage.

7—Group Discussion (5–7 minutes)

The facilitator invites insights from the whole group. This is *not* a teaching moment—listen, affirm, and summarize.

Non-negotiables for ETHNOS Group Discussions

- Always include **1 minute of silence.**
- Always include **partner sharing.**
- Always include a **group discussion.**

You may flex the time depending on your context, but *do not skip the process.*

A Note for Youth Facilitators

ETHNOS has proven to be deeply impactful for students ages **twelve to fifteen** when it is facilitated with clarity, simplicity, and intentional structure. Adolescents at this stage are forming their worldview, learning to articulate what they believe, and beginning to notice cultural and religious differences around them. ETHNOS meets them at exactly the right moment—*when curiosity is high, and courage is still forming.*

This section is written specifically for *church leaders, youth pastors,* and *small-group facilitators* guiding middle-school and early high-school students through ETHNOS.

What Works Best for Ages 12–15

Through years of piloting ETHNOS with teenagers, we have learned that *less is more* for this age group.

For students ages twelve to fifteen, the most fruitful weekly rhythm includes *only the following three element*s during the group session:

1. **Watch the video together.**
2. **Use the Group Discussion questions.**
3. **Spend time in Scripture and the "I Will" statement.**

Students do *not* need to read every section of the coursebook during the live session. Nor do they need all background explanations, extended religious comparisons, or every example in the coursebook.

They *do* need:

- space to talk,
- permission to ask honest questions,
- time to reflect quietly how they might apply concepts in their lives,
- and encouragement to take simple steps of obedience.

For this age group, the coursebook is best used as:

- a **guide**,
- a **reflection space**, and
- a **take-home companion** for students who want to go deeper outside of group time.

Youth Facilitation Tips

- Prevent adults from dominating discussion.
- Use the 1-2-4-7 method faithfully. It is especially powerful with teens.
- Normalize uncertainty. Growth comes from curiosity, not confidence.
- Shorter answers are better than longer explanations.

If youth leaders follow the session flow and protect discussion time, *God does the rest*.

ETHNOS Session Flow

A Simple, Proven Rhythm for a 60–90 Minute Group

Total Session Time Options

- **60 minutes**—streamlined
- **90 minutes**—ideal, maximum processing

Participants will not read the full coursebook during group time. The coursebook supports before and after, not everything during.

1. WELCOME AND PRAYER (10–15 minutes)

Purpose: Set tone, build safety, invite God's presence.

What to Do

- Welcome everyone warmly
- Brief opening prayer

(Optional) A quick check-in question or two, such as *Where have you noticed God at work this week?* or *How have you practiced your "I will" statement?*

> **TIP**
> Keep this light. Avoid teaching or summarizing last week.

2. WATCH THE VIDEO (<15 minutes)

Purpose: Let the video do the teaching.

What to Do

- Play the ETHNOS session video in full.
- Ask participants to listen for:
  - what stands out.
  - what challenges them.
  - what feels practical.

> **TIP**
> Do *not* pre-teach or preview the content. The video is the authority, not the facilitator.

3. 1-2-4-7 DISCUSSION (10–20 minutes)

The 1-2-4-7 Discussion Method is the core transformation engine for this group study.

1—Silent Processing (1 minute)

A time for personal reflection before group influence. This quiet minute is where *self-awareness and conviction begin.*

What to Do

- Ask participants to silently reflect on the *Think It Through* questions at the end of each chapter.
- Encourage brief notes in the coursebook.

2—Partner Sharing (2 minutes)

Participants share their thoughts with one person.

4—Small Group Sharing (4 minutes)

Two pairs combine to create groups of four to discuss thoughts, questions, or discoveries.

7—Whole Group Debrief (5–7 minutes)

Facilitator draws out insights from the whole group.

Purpose

- Everyone speaks.
- No one dominates.
- The Holy Spirit works through shared processing.

Facilitator Tips

- Ask open-ended questions.
- Affirm participation.
- Redirect gently if someone begins teaching or storytelling excessively.

> **REMINDER: THE 1-2-4-7 DISCUSSION METHOD IS ESSENTIAL.**
> *DO NOT SKIP IT.*

4. Read and Process Scripture (15 Minutes)

Purpose: Let God's Word do the deep work.

What to Do

- Invite participants to silently read the assigned scripture(s) and circle one to ponder.
- Use the provided questions to process the scriptures individually first and then as a group.
- Use the full **1-2-4-7 discussion method** if time allows. *If you are short on time, allow time for partner sharing and group debrief at a minimum.*

> **FACILITATOR TIP**
>
> Don't explain the scripture. Let participants wrestle with it and respond.

5. "I Will" Statement (5 minutes)

Purpose: Move from insight to obedience.

What to Do

- Ask participants to write one clear, actionable "I will" statement.
- Pair up and share statements.

Examples

- *I will pray with one person this week in Jesus' name.*
- *I will identify myself as a follower of Jesus early in conversations.*

6. Closing Prayer and Next Steps (5 minutes)

Purpose: Seal commitment and build expectancy.

What to Do

- Invite someone to pray over the group.

- Invite participants to . . .
  - activate their "I will" statement,
  - work through the session in the coursebook on their own,
  - refer to additional iHOPE resources for deeper learning,
  - come ready to share next session, and
  - bring a friend.
- **Optional:** Share a short testimony or encouragement (30–60 seconds max)

Time Summary	
Segment	*Time*
Welcome and Prayer	10–15 min
Video	15 min
Group Discussion	10–20 min
Scripture Processing	10–20 min
"I Will" Statement	10–15 min
Next Steps and Closing Prayer	5 min
Total	**60–90 min**

Final Facilitator Encouragement

ETHNOS is not about doing everything right. It is about abiding in Jesus, being **available, obedient,** and **authentic.** You don't need to fill silence, answer every question, or impress the group.

Your role as an ETHNOS facilitator is simple:

- create space
- protect the process
- point people back to Jesus

If you follow the flow, protect discussion, and keep Jesus at the center, you are facilitating well. More importantly, when you do that, **God does the rest**.

God delights in using ordinary believers to accomplish extraordinary things.

ETHNOS Facilitator Covenant

As an ETHNOS facilitator, you are a guide. Trust the video. Trust the process. Trust the Holy Spirit. We encourage you to join other group leaders worldwide in taking this posture and making the ETHNOS Facilitator Covenant to help ensure the success of your group:

I will create space rather than try to control outcomes.

I will listen more than I speak.

I will honor every voice.

I will protect Scripture and reflection time.

I will trust the Holy Spirit to do the work I cannot do.

THE FOUNDATION

> All the nations you have made will come and worship before you, Lord; they will bring glory to your name.
>
> —PSALM 86:9, NIV

A spiritual battle is unfolding all around us—one that impacts every human soul.

Scripture is clear that this is not a war of flesh and blood, but a spiritual one (Ephesians 6:12). It has been raging since creation, and it continues today in neighborhoods, workplaces, classrooms, and homes across the world.

Most people are not hostile to God. They are searching, wondering, and longing—often without the language to name it. And yet, many have never clearly heard who Jesus is or why he matters.

God has always worked through ordinary people to make himself known. Not experts. Not professionals. Just faithful believers of all ages who were willing to take the next step of obedience. Now it's your turn.

WATCH THE VIDEO: THE FOUNDATION

Access the video teaching lessons by going to EthnosCourse.org, and logging in to your account.

Tip: ETHNOS Course video lessons are also available through RightNow Media.

After you've watched the video, take a moment to reflect on what you saw and heard.

What stood out to you most from this short video?

What challenged or stretched you?

What felt hopeful or encouraging?

Consider what God is asking of you. What are God's three primary purposes for you, as seen in the video?

A STORY THAT ILLUSTRATES THE STAKES

Min and Nanda May lived with their three young children in a country marked by political instability, violence, and poverty. Christians lived nearby, yet none told them about hope in Jesus.

One night, war suddenly reached their town. Min was taken by force to fight. Nanda fled on foot with her children, eventually reaching a refugee camp in another country. Sadly, Min never returned. He died in the conflict.

Christian volunteers in the refugee camp shared the gospel with Nanda. She came to faith in Jesus and committed to raising her children to follow him.

As she grew in her understanding of Scripture, Nanda began asking painful questions.

What is going to happen to my husband on Judgement Day? What will be his destination, heaven or hell?

He never heard about Jesus. Why didn't anyone tell us?

Her questions were deeply personal—and eternal.

The May family's story is a physical picture of a spiritual reality. A war is raging, and people are affected whether they are aware or not.

Think It Through

Allow yourself time to prayerfully consider the following questions. Notice how the Holy Spirit might be leading your thoughts.

When and how did you first hear the gospel?

_____

_____

_____

Do you believe that Jesus is the hope of the world? How have your actions lined up with your thoughts?

_____

_____

_____

What holds your friends back from sharing Jesus with nonbelievers—especially those from other faiths and cultures?

_____
_____
_____
_____

What, if anything, has held you back from sharing Jesus with people who don't know him?

_____
_____
_____
_____

Group Discussion

Observe Together

- Introduce yourself and share what prompted you to join this study. Share how you hope to grow through it.
- Pick a Think It Through question and share your reflections with the group.
- If you are leading a group through this study, look for discussion guidelines in the front of this coursebook.

Read and Process Scripture

Each session, you will read and process scriptures that amplify concepts in the lesson. Read the following verses. Circle one that you would like to contemplate.

> "If you love me, you will keep my commandments."
>
> —JOHN 14:15, NASB

> How then are they to call on Him in whom they have not believed? How are they to believe in Him whom they have not heard?
>
> —ROMANS 10:14A, NASB

> For so the Lord has commanded us, "I have appointed you as a light to the gentiles, that you may bring salvation to the end of the earth."
>
> —ACTS 13:47, NASB

> Therefore, we are ambassadors for Christ, as though God were making an appeal through us.
>
> —2 CORINTHIANS 5:20A, NASB

> "Behold, I am coming quickly, and My reward *is* with Me, to reward each one as his work deserves. I am the Alpha and the Omega, the first and the last, the beginning and the end."
>
> —REVELATION 22:12–13, NASB

Which verse did you pick? Contemplate the verse by considering these questions:

What does this verse make you think or feel? Why?

What does this verse tell you about God?

What does this verse tell you about you and your relationship with God?

_____
_____
_____

What actions do you think God wants from you based on this passage?

_____
_____
_____

Your "I Will" Statement

What do you think the Holy Spirit is prompting you to think about or do differently based on what you learned? Write an "I will…" statement that you want to focus on this week in response to this prompting. *Example: "I will pray that the Lord opens the eyes of my heart to see people around me who don't know Jesus."*

This week, I will . . .

_____
_____
_____
_____

Next Steps

- ○ If you are doing this study in a group, pair up with someone and share your "I will" statement.
- ○ Commit to practicing your "I will" statement throughout the week ahead.
- ○ Come ready to share how you activated your "I will" statement at the next session.
- ○ There is still time to invite a friend to join you in this study. Who would you like to invite? Write that person's name below and reach out to them this week.

Closing Prayer

Lord, help me to "see" people from many nations around me who do not know you. What do you want me to know about them? What do you want me to do? I pray that you will deepen my faith through this study and give me a fresh boldness to share it.

Looking Ahead

The spiritual war you explored in this session is not distant or abstract. It is unfolding all around you. God does not leave his people unprepared or alone in this calling.

In the next session, you will be equipped to overcome one of the greatest barriers that keep many believers from stepping into this calling: *fear*—fear of not knowing enough, fear of saying the wrong thing, fear of being rejected. And you will discover why fear does not get the final word.

SESSION 1

UNDERSTANDING WORLD RELIGIONS

> **WATCH THE VIDEO: UNDERSTANDING WORLD RELIGIONS**

Take a moment to reflect on what you just watched.

What stood out to you most from this video?

What challenged or stretched you?

What felt hopeful or encouraging?

Why This Session Matters

Most believers genuinely want others to know Jesus—yet feel unsure where to begin, what to say, or how to engage people whose beliefs feel unfamiliar.

This session will help you overcome these obstacles.

You will begin to see the world the way Jesus did: not as a collection of intimidating belief systems, but as people—created in God's image—who are searching for truth, meaning, and hope. You will gain a simple, working understanding of what your neighbors, coworkers, classmates, and friends from other faiths believe about God, Jesus, salvation, and the afterlife.

More importantly, you will discover that being prepared does not mean knowing everything. It means knowing *him*.

This session is designed to broaden your perspective, deepen compassion for nonbelievers, and replace fear with quiet confidence as you step into your calling to be an authentic witness for Jesus at school, work, and in your neighborhood.

Are You Prepared?

One of the most common reasons Christians hesitate to start conversation that could lead to Jesus is this:

"I don't know how."

We assume we need more biblical knowledge, more cultural awareness, or more training before we can engage people of other faiths. Yet when Jesus sent his followers into the world—across nations, cultures, and religions—he did not enroll them in a course on world religions first.

They didn't have search engines.

They did not have scripts or charts.

They didn't have access to endless information.

What they had was *Jesus*.

Jesus knew his disciples didn't need to know everything about the people they were going to meet. They needed to know *him*—and to walk closely with God.

> **A STORY FROM REAL LIFE**
>
> Jack was a successful corporate executive who deeply desired to share Jesus with Muslims. But there was a problem: he felt completely unprepared. He didn't know enough about Islam.
>
> So, Jack did what any motivated Christian would do—he studied.
>
> And studied.
>
> And studied some more.
>
> For three years, Jack immersed himself in learning everything he could about Islam and Muslim culture. Yet the more he learned, the more he realized how much he *did not* know. His confidence didn't grow—it shrank.
>
> Eventually, though still unsure, Jack decided it was time to engage.
>
> Through his work, Jack met a man named Fady. Assuming Fady was Muslim, Jack initiated a spiritual conversation. But Jack quickly discovered that Fady wasn't Muslim at all. In fact, Fady followed a religion Jack had never heard of—and knew nothing about.
>
> In that moment, Jack remembered Jesus' original followers.
>
> Jesus sent them into the world with far less information than he had. Jesus had not trained them in the details of other belief systems. He had trained them to depend on God.
>
> With no expertise to rely on, Jack leaned on the same biblical principles you will learn in this session—and throughout the ETHNOS course.
>
> Those principles worked.
>
> Within a year of that first conversation, Fady became a follower of Jesus.

Following Jesus prepared the disciples to tell others about him.

It prepares you too.

You don't need to be an expert in world religions.

You don't need to be an apologist, theologian, or exceptional evangelist.

You just need to abide in Jesus—and follow the model he gave.

> *"I realized that I don't have to be a Bible expert.
> I just have to share the love of Jesus."*
>
> **—ETHNOS student**

How Jesus Prepared His Followers

Jesus prepared his disciples in four simple, powerful ways. These same four principles will prepare you today.

1. Know Scripture

Throughout his ministry, Jesus consistently referred to Scripture. In fact, the phrase "It is written" appears or is alluded to more than ninety times in the New Testament.

Scripture anchors you in truth and reveals who God is.

> And beginning with Moses and all the Prophets, He explained to them what was said in all the Scriptures concerning Himself.
>
> —LUKE 24:27, NIV

Knowing Scripture does not mean memorizing entire books of the Bible. It means becoming familiar with God's Word and knowing where to turn when questions arise.

Jack was not gifted at Scripture memorization. Yet he learned how to use the tools available to him—Bible apps, keyword searches, and concordances—to quickly find what Scripture says about topics like God, sin, salvation, and Jesus.

You can do the same.

Understanding the Gospel

What is the gospel? In your own words, write out the good news about Jesus.

_____
_____
_____
_____
_____

Read each passage below. In your own words, summarize what these verses communicate about the gospel.

- John 3:16
- John 14:6
- Acts 4:12
- Romans 3:21–26
- Romans 10:9–11
- 1 John 5:12

_____
_____
_____
_____
_____
_____
_____
_____
_____

2. Have a Relationship with God Through Jesus Christ

Preparation begins with relationship.

Jack didn't engage Fady because of confidence in his knowledge—he was compelled by his love for Christ. As Scripture says, *"Christ's love compels us"* (2 Corinthians 5:14 NIV).

> "No one has ever seen God, but the one and only Son, who is Himself God and is in closest relationship with the Father, has made Him known."
>
> —JOHN 1:18 NIV

Jesus reveals God to us—and invites us into relationship.

> **READ COLOSSIANS 1:15–23.**

What do these verses tell you about Jesus?

_____
_____
_____
_____

What do they reveal about your relationship with God?

_____
_____
_____
_____

3. Be Empowered by the Holy Spirit

Jesus never sent his followers out alone.

> "But you will receive power when the Holy Spirit comes on you; and you will be My witnesses..."
>
> —ACTS 1:8A, NIV

God has already given you everything you need: his Word and his Spirit.

When Jack realized he didn't understand Fady's beliefs, he leaned not on his education—but on the Holy Spirit. God gave him wisdom, courage, and discernment in real time.

Read the following passages.

- John 14:16–17, 26
- Matthew 10:19–20
- Romans 8:11
- 2 Timothy 1:6–7
- Romans 8:26

How are you empowered by the Holy Spirit?

Begin to Practice This Rhythm

- **Ask** the Holy Spirit to guide you.
- **Listen** for his leading.
- **Respond** in obedience.

4. Engage with People of Other Faiths and Cultures

Jesus intentionally took his disciples into places that felt uncomfortable and unfamiliar—Tyre, Sidon, and the Decapolis—so they would meet people of other faiths.

You don't have to travel overseas to meet people from other faiths and cultures. Where might you meet them here?

FROM MUSLIM TO CHRISTIAN: JOURNEY OF FAITH AND TRANSFORMATION

"When I was filled with that joy, I wanted to tell the whole world about Jesus. I couldn't understand how I'm going to do it. I wasn't trained. I only knew what I felt and what happened to me, and that had to be done to the universe."

Narmin grew up in a Muslim family in a Soviet nation, where talking about God was prohibited, but she sensed that there was something beyond the material world. You can hear her story and others like it on The Blue Cord, by iHOPE Ministries podcast. Available wherever you listen to podcasts.

TheBlueCord.org

What Do Your Neighbors Believe?

What different religions believe about …	Christianity	Islam	Hinduism	Buddhism	Spiritual	Secular
God	One triune God	One God, no Trinity	Brahma plus millions of gods	An abstract void	Impersonal divine oneness	None
Jesus	God, the Son	Prophet, not God	Teacher, a god	Teacher	Teacher	Teacher
Salvation	Jesus	Muslim plus good works	Spiritual growth to knowledge and wisdom	Spiritual growth to selflessness	Spiritual growth to enlightenment	None
After Life	Heaven or Hell	Paradise or Hell	Merge into divinity	Nirvana, selfless existence	Divine universal oneness	None
Denominations	Many	Many	Many	Many	Many	Many

Tip

To learn more about engaging with Muslims, read *Muslims: 5 Essentials Christians should Know and Do* by Renod Bejjani.

Think It Through

As you consider the following questions, notice how the Holy Spirit might be leading your thoughts and actions:

Given the rise of globalization, what opportunities do you see for Christians?

Where might you meet people of other faiths in your community?

How do you see the decline of a biblical worldview impacting you, your family, and your nation?

Do you believe Jesus is the hope of the world? How have your actions lined up with your thoughts?

Group Discussion

Observe Together

- Share an aha moment you've had since you last got together.
- Share how you have been practicing your "I will" statement from the previous session.
- Pick a Think It Through question from this session to reflect on with the group.

Read and Process Scripture

Read the following verses and select one that you would like to contemplate:

> This is good and acceptable in the sight of God our Savior, who wants all people to be saved and to come to the knowledge of the truth.
>
> —1 TIMOTHY 2:3–4, NASB

> "The one who is not with Me is against Me, and the one who does not gather with Me scatters."
>
> —LUKE 11:23, NASB

> So Jesus said to them again, "Peace be to you; just as the Father has sent Me, I also send you."
>
> —JOHN 20:21, NASB

> For so the Lord has commanded us: "I have appointed you as a light to the Gentiles, that you may bring salvation to the end of the earth."
>
> —ACTS 13:47, NASB

> And He said to them, "Go into all the world and preach the gospel to all creation."
>
> —MARK 16:15, NASB

Which verse did you pick and why?

What does this verse make you think or feel? Why?

What does it tell you about God?

What does it tell you about your relationship with God?

What actions do you think God wants from you based on this passage?

Your "I Will" Statement

What might the Holy Spirit be prompting you to think about or do differently this week based on what you learned? Write an "I will" statement that you want to focus on doing this week in response to this prompting.

_____
_____
_____
_____
_____
_____
_____
_____
_____

Next Steps

- ○ Pair up with someone and share your statement.
- ○ Commit to practicing your "I will" statement this week. Be ready to share in the next group gathering what the Lord has been teaching you.
- ○ Tell a friend about any ETHNOS concepts that are resonating with you right now.

Closing Prayer

Journal a short prayer for your week ahead.

SESSION 2

START SPIRITUAL CONVERSATIONS

WATCH THE VIDEO: START SPIRITUAL CONVERSATIONS

Take a moment to reflect on what you just watched.

What stood out to you most from this video?

What challenged or stretched you?

What felt hopeful or encouraging?

Session Overview

God has brought people from all over the world to us. You don't have to travel far to meet someone from a culture or belief system that is different from yours.

Finding people to tell about Jesus is rarely the problem.

More often, what keeps most willing Christians from sharing Jesus is *knowing what to say and how to say it*. Bringing up faith can seem risky, rude, or simply awkward. So, we kindly smile and make polite small talk.

This session will equip you to shift from polite small talk *to initiating meaningful spiritual conversations* that can lead to Jesus.

What Gets in the Way

Much of our fear exists because of the human tendency to rely on self rather than God. It's human nature to want to be self-reliant and self-sufficient.

Look at the chart below that compares the self-focused human way of witness to the approach that relies on God's way.

Human Way Versus God's Way

Human Way	God's Way
"If I do _____ (fill in the blank), better and/or longer, then I'm more likely to see him/her come to Christ."	"If I'm seeking God and practicing Biblical truths in my daily life, then I'm more likely to see him/her come to Christ."
• Perfect my testimony • Perfect gospel methods • Know all about religions • Know what *not* to do • Handle every objection	• Seek God for help • Pray for discernment • Listen for Holy Spirit guidance • Read the Bible • Live out 5 Christian principles

Human Way

Before I can share Jesus with others, I must . . .

- perfect my testimony
- perfect gospel methods
- know all about other religions
- know what *not* to do
- handle every objection

God's Way

If I am seeking God and practicing biblical truths in my daily life, then God can use me to bring others to Christ. I . . .

- seek God for help
- pray for discernment
- listen for the Holy Spirit's guidance
- study the Bible
- live out five Christian principles (These will be discussed in detail in the next session.)

Personal Reflection

Which of the human-way statements do you most relate to?

How have those concerns or beliefs inhibited you from talking about Jesus with others?

Fill in the blank for yourself:

If I _____, then I'm more likely to see him/her come to Christ.

Abiding Produces Fruit

Read John 15:1–5. What does it mean to bear fruit?

_____
_____
_____
_____

How do Christians bear fruit?

_____
_____
_____
_____

Look at verses 4 and 5. Is it possible to do this on your own?

_____
_____
_____
_____

Self-reliance is the opposite of how you are called to live as an authentic witness. Relying on God's leading and abiding in Jesus are essential, not optional for Christ-followers.

> Trust in and rely confidently on the Lord with all your heart
> and do not rely on your own insight or understanding.
>
> —PROVERBS 3:5, AMP

3 Ground Rules to Being an Authentic Christian Witness

In addition to relying on God and abiding in Jesus, keep these three ground rules:

1. Be an intentional ambassador for Christ.

> We are therefore Christ's ambassadors, as though God were making his appeal through us.
>
> —2 CORINTHIANS 5:20, NIV

Look up the word *ambassador.* **In your own words, write what it means to be an ambassador of Christ.**

_____

_____

_____

_____

Read 2 Corinthians 5:18–21. What task or ministry has God assigned to us as ambassadors of Jesus?

_____

_____

_____

_____

2. Expect divine appointments.

Everywhere you go—the grocery store, the dentist, to work, school, or the park—there are people all around you who don't know Jesus. As an ambassador of Christ, you are his representative to the nations.

Read Luke 10:1–3, NIV. What does Jesus tell his disciples?

_____

_____

_____

After this the Lord appointed seventy-two others and sent them two by two ahead of him to every town and place where _____ was _____ to _____. He told them, "The harvest is plentiful, but the workers are few. Ask the Lord of the harvest, therefore, to send out workers into his harvest field. _____! I am sending _____ out like lambs among wolves."

Why did Jesus send his disciples ahead of him?

Jesus told his disciples to pray that the Lord of the Harvest, God, would send workers. Then Jesus immediately sends his disciples on a mission. They were the answer to that prayer.

God has brought the nations to you, and just as Jesus promised the seventy-two, he will be right behind you. As a follower of Jesus and his ambassador, you are given the same task—to help prepare the way for him by sharing the good news.

What did Jesus mean when he said the harvest is plentiful?

God was not waiting for the disciples. He was already at work in the places they would go.

The same is true for us today. God is already at work in the hearts and lives of our other-faith neighbors. Many of them are ready to hear about Jesus. They just need someone to make the introduction. They are not far from him because you are there.

3. Tithe your time.

> "Seek the Kingdom of God above all else, and live righteously,
> and he will give you everything you need."
>
> —MATTHEW 6:33, NLT

The third ground rule to being an authentic witness for Jesus is to be intentional with your time. When Jesus is Lord of your life, everything you have, including your time, belongs to God. Prioritizing your offerings of time, just as you do with your financial tithes, honors God.

It is easy to get busy with work, family life, hobbies, even church activities. None of those things are bad or wrong. The goal is to be intentional about building God's kingdom by sharing what matters most—Jesus and the salvation he offers.

Tips for Time Tithing

Even if you are busy, you can make this part of your everyday life by putting yourself in situations where you are likely to encounter people of other faiths and cultures.

- Shop at an ethnic grocery store where families of other cultures live.
- Eat at an ethnic restaurant where you are likely to run into people of other faiths.
- Volunteer to serve refugees, immigrants, or international students.

Where are you most likely to encounter people of other faiths and cultures?

What If I Say the Wrong Thing?

We all want to be successful when we share our Christian faith. No one wants to fail. Often, however, that desire leads believers to put burdens on themselves before opening their mouths for Jesus.

Have you ever thought any of the following?

> *We do good works and hope that our loving deeds will woo others to Jesus.*
>
> *We drop hints about our Christian faith and hope people will ask questions.*
>
> *We build relationships on everything but Christ and hope the topic of Jesus will one-day surface naturally.*

The problem is that when *we* do these things, and no one asks us about Jesus, it seems awkward to bring him up.

But there is hope. Start by praying for boldness and use this sample script to eliminate any tension you might feel.

Words to Say

"I'm excited to know you, to learn about your beliefs and culture. Until I know those things, I don't want to offend you by saying or doing something inappropriate. Will you promise to forgive me if I do that and teach me so I don't do it again?"

Take Your Learning Deeper

Read Acts 3 and 4 and consider what it means to boldly share your faith and model that for your family.

Who was offended by Peter and John, and why?

How did Peter and John respond in 4:8–12?

What did people notice about Peter and John (see 4:13–14)?

What stands out to you in the believers' prayer in 4:23–30?

How did God respond to the believers' prayer (see 4:31)?

The Holy Spirit is in you. Ask God. He will give you the boldness to share the love and truth of Jesus.

Practice Salty Speech

> Be wise in the way you act toward outsiders; make the most of every opportunity. Let your conversation be always full of grace, seasoned with salt, so that you may know how to answer everyone.
>
> —COLOSSIANS 4:5–6, NIV

Engaging people in spiritual conversations is simpler than you imagine.

1. Start by offering a little information about yourself.
2. Add some "salty speech" with a spiritual hook.
3. Then, ask a question.

The FORM acronym is a great place to start when you aren't sure what to say. Adding salty speech with a spiritual hook allows you to purposefully move the conversation toward spiritual things.

Review the bolded spiritual hooks in the examples below and then write your own conversation starter based on your life and experiences.

FORM Conversations Starters		
Topic	**Example**	**Your Turn**
Friends and Family	We have five sons. **I am grateful that three are walking closely with God.** How about you? Any kids?	
Occupation and Education	My favorite job is being an **ambassador for God**. For work, I am in the tech field. How about you? What do you do for a living? I'm studying business because I want to help oppressed women succeed. I've found that happens best **through a relationship with Jesus**. How about you? What are you studying?	
Religion and Recreation	I love to hike on weekends because when I'm in nature, **I feel closer to God**. What do you like to do on the weekend?	
Me	We just moved here **because God impressed it on our hearts**. How about you? Where are you originally from?	

STORY: LUCAS AND MEHDI

Lucas didn't have to travel around the world to reach people who didn't know Jesus. His coworker Mehdi was a Muslim from the Middle East. They were both avid bikers and rode together after work a couple days a week.

The problem was that Lucas didn't know how to bring up Jesus. He was comfortable talking about work, his family, even politics. Yet bring up Jesus? Well, that seemed risky, awkward, and just plain rude.

So Lucas hid his faith from Mehdi for three years and held on to these fears:

- Fear of saying the wrong thing
- Fear of offending the other person
- Fear of not having all the answers
- Fear of being rejected
- Fear of being labeled as intolerant

> For God has not given us a spirit of fear and timidity, but of power, love, and self-discipline.
>
> —2 TIMOTHY 1:7, NLT

When Lucas heard about ETHNOS, he took the study at his church—hoping God would help him move beyond these fears. When he discovered the FORM acronym, he crafted a conversation starter he could use with Mehdi.

You won't believe what happened next.

"Mehdi, one of my favorite things about riding my bike in nature is that *I feel closer to God*. How about you? Besides the exercise, what do you enjoy about riding your bike in nature?"

Lucas was shocked by Mehdi's answer.

"Lucas, we've known each other for three years. You know I'm Muslim, and I've talked about my faith many times, but you never mentioned God before. Are you a Christian? I thought that faith was not important to you."

Lucas felt embarrassed, but responded with the paragraph he practiced:

"My faith is really important to me. I was afraid that what I believe might offend you, so I didn't bring it up."

How do you think Mehdi responded?

Mehdi asked questions about what Christians believe, and they ended up talking about spiritual things for over an hour. That was only the beginning. Now, a couple of years since that encounter, Mehdi is studying the Bible with Lucas. I pray that by the time you're reading this, Mehdi has become a follower of Jesus.

For Lucas to begin a spiritual conversation with his coworker Mehdi—and with people of other faiths—he felt he had to be better equipped with all five categories in the list under the Human Way heading. Lucas's biggest fear was offending Mehdi. And as an engineer, he also wanted to do things "right" so that he could achieve spiritual fruit with Mehdi.

Think It Through

Which of the 3 Ground Rules most resonates with you? Why?

_____
_____
_____

Write out and practice saying a FORM Conversation starter of your own.

_____
_____
_____
_____
_____

Now that you know how to start spiritual conversations, are you willing to put yourself out there and practice?

_____
_____
_____
_____
_____

Group Discussion

Observe Together

- Share how you have been practicing your "I will" statement.
- Pick a Think It Through question from this session to reflect on with the group.

Read and Process Scripture

Read each of the following verses. Circle one that connects with, encourages, or convicts you. Contemplate the scriptures for a few moments.

> "My Father is glorified by this, that you bear much fruit, and so prove to be My disciples."
>
> —JOHN 15:8, NASB
>
> Your speech must always be with grace, as though seasoned with salt, so that you will know how you should respond to each person.
>
> —COLOSSIANS 4:6, NASB
>
> Preach the word; be ready in season and out of season; correct, rebuke, and exhort, with great patience and instruction.
>
> —2 TIMOTHY 4:2, NASB
>
> And I pray that the fellowship of your faith may become effective through the knowledge of every good thing which is in you for the sake of Christ.
>
> —PHILEMON 1:6, NASB

Which verse did you pick? Contemplate the verse by considering these questions.

What does this verse make you think or feel? Why?

What does it tell you about God?

What does it tell you about your relationship with God?

What actions do you think God wants from you based on this passage?

Your "I Will" Statement

What might the Holy Spirit be prompting you to think about or do differently this week? Write an "I will" statement that you want to focus on in response to this prompting.

I will . . .

Next Steps

- Pair up with someone and share your "I will" statement.
- Write out a FORM statement of your own.
- Tell a friend about any ETHNOS concepts that are resonating with you right now.
- Activate your "I will" statement this week.
- Come ready to share how you activated your "I will" statement at the next session.

Closing Prayer

Journal a short prayer for your week ahead.

SESSION 3

THE 5 ESSENTIALS + LOVE

WATCH THE VIDEO: THE 5 ESSENTIALS + LOVE

Reflect on what you heard in the video.

What stood out to you most from the video?

_____
_____
_____
_____

What challenged or stretched you?

_____
_____
_____
_____

What felt hopeful or encouraging?

_____
_____
_____
_____

Session Overview

In the previous session, you learned how to confidently start spiritual conversations with anyone, anywhere, all the time.

Once you start those conversations, what do you do next?

This session answers that question. You will be armed with a foundational overview of "The 5 Essentials"—five ways to live as an authentic witness among other-faith coworkers, classmates, and neighbors in your everyday life.

> Instead, you must worship Christ as Lord of your life. And if someone asks about your hope as a believer, always be ready to explain it.
>
> —1 PETER 3:15, NLT

The 5 Essentials

1.	2.	3.	4.	5.
Love in words, actions, and deeds.	Look for a person of peace.	Pray together, in Jesus' name.	Share the gospel, early and often.	Share the Bible.

These 5 Essentials are actions and attitudes Jesus modeled—and they've been effective for centuries. They are simple, practical ways to live as an authentic Christian witness in your everyday life.

Since 2011, iHOPE Ministries' participants have used the 5 Essentials to share Jesus with hundreds of thousands of people from other faith backgrounds. We've witnessed life-changing results—for both the believer and the person meeting Jesus for the first time or encountering him in a new and authentic way.

Abiding Is Not Optional

The 5 Essentials work together—and **all five are necessary**. But they only bear fruit when you are **abiding in Jesus**.

Read John 15:4–5, NKJV. Fill in the blanks with the words of Jesus:

"_____ in Me, and I in you. As the branch cannot bear fruit of itself, unless it abides in the vine, neither can you, unless you _____ in _____. I am the vine, you are the branches. He who _____ in Me, and I in him, bears much fruit; for without _____ you can do nothing."

Essential 1: Love in Words, Actions, and Deeds

The 5 Essentials work because they reflect the heart of Jesus. And **love is where everything begins**.

Nonbelievers are drawn to Jesus when they experience the love of Christ flowing through a Christian friend *within the context of an authentic relationship*.

Why is love more appealing as it flows through us in the context of a relationship?

_____

_____

_____

_____

_____

The Greatest Commandment

Read Matthew 22:37–40. What is the greatest commandment?

_____

_____

_____

_____

What does Jesus say about the second greatest commandment in verses 39–40?

_____

_____

_____

When Love Isn't Easy

> Greater is He who is in you than he who is in the world.
> —1 JOHN 4:4, NASB

Faulty Assumptions—Loving someone who thinks, believes, or behaves differently from you isn't always easy. Fears, misunderstandings, assumptions, and misconceptions can quietly shape attitudes—sometimes without realizing the lack of love in our own hearts.

What assumptions or fears do you have about people of other faiths that might be holding you back from sharing Christ with them?

_____

_____

_____

Fighting for Jesus—Sometimes Christians try to persuade others to believe in Jesus—arguments replace relationship, and love gets lost. When conversations turn combative, love is missing.

Read John 13:35. What does Jesus say is the defining characteristic of his disciples?

_____

_____

_____

_____

Be Filled with God's Love

Read 1 John 4:7. What is the source of love?

Being filled with God's love is what enables you to love others well—in words, actions, and deeds. Remember: being an ambassador of Jesus isn't about what *you* can do or say to convince someone. It is about what Jesus does through you.

Read 1 Corinthians 13. What does love do?

What does love not do?

Why is love greater than faith and hope?

Considering these verses, how can you love others well in words, actions, and deeds?

Sharing God's Love Across Faiths

People from other faiths often do not have a relational understanding of God. In Islam, Allah is not love and does not enter personal relationship with humanity. In Hinduism, Buddhism, and many forms of New Age spirituality, there is no relational being at all.

In contrast, Christians believe God created humankind in his image as an act of love. *God created us for relationship with him.* Not only is God love—*he loves us.*

Read John 3:16–17. How do Jesus' words contrast with what other religions believe about God and his relationship with humanity?

_____

_____

_____

God is love, and he created a need within each of us to be loved. When people from other faiths discover that God desires a relationship with them and loves them personally, it is deeply compelling.

ASMA'S STORY

I grew up in an Arab country that is 99 percent Muslim. My family are all devout Muslims. God was a master and I feared him. When I was nine, I finished fasting during Ramadan for the first time. It was a great accomplishment.

When I came to the United States as an international student, my family was afraid that I would be influenced by the Christian culture. They were concerned that I would become rebellious and live a sinful life. I don't really blame them because what they saw in the media would scare any parent.

The first time I met true followers of Jesus, I realized my perception about Christians wasn't true. My Christian friends were kind and loving. They told me about God's love and what it meant to have a relationship with God. This was a mind-blowing concept to me. I couldn't comprehend it. What does it mean that God loves me unconditionally? I couldn't imagine not having to do anything to gain God's love. It was the opposite of everything that I knew as a Muslim.

When my Christian friends told me Jesus was God, I considered it blasphemy, a sure ticket to hell. I loved my friends and I didn't want them to go to hell, so I set out to convert them to Islam. Even though their salvation couldn't be assured, I figured they had a better chance by being Muslim.

To convert my friends, I had to study Islam deeply. Through that study, the Lord began opening my eyes to things I never noticed before. I said, "God if you are in Islam, then keep me in it. If you are somewhere else, show me."

Then God gave me the desire to read the Bible. No Christian had given me a Bible and I didn't want to ask for one because I'd been telling my friends it had been corrupted. So, I took one from a Christian friend without their permission. It was the best bad thing I've ever done. I started reading it from the beginning.

Soon I started seeing what all my Christian friends were talking about—the crazy unconditional love of God. God revealed himself to me as I studied his word. It was a beautiful thing knowing I was forgiven and loved by God. I accepted Jesus as my Lord and Savior.

—Asma

DILDORA'S STORY

I grew up in a non-Christian household. My parents never expressed their love for me, my siblings, or each other when I was growing up. My father was abusive—physically and emotionally. I watched my mom struggle with my father. It made me hate my dad.

Our family would often hang out with six other families in the neighborhood. One day, one of those families accepted Christ, and whenever they would come to the neighborhood gatherings, they would always talk about Jesus. The other families got frustrated with that. They would say, "If you want to continue hanging out with us, leave Jesus at home and come by yourself." In time, that Christian family stopped coming because they were not welcomed.

About eight years passed. I had forgotten all about that family. My parents were away, and my sister and I were home alone. The doorbell rang. It was that same Christian family. They had come to visit us. We welcomed them in and put out tea and sweets. Soon they started telling us about Jesus.

They shared a verse in the Bible that really touched my heart. It said something about God showing his great love for us by sending Christ to die for us while we were still sinners. Hearing that Jesus died because he loved me? Well, that was incredible because I was always desperate for my parents' love. The verse just blew me away. I couldn't get enough of it. I wanted to know, "God loves me? Really?"

I accepted Jesus as my Lord and Savior that day. After that, God healed my heart from the bitterness and anger I had long felt toward my abusive father. In time, I shared Jesus with him. Turns out, he'd never known love either. My father had witnessed such an incredible change in me that he wanted to be transformed by the love of Christ too.

—Dildora

Think It Through

Why is love not enough?

Why is love more appealing as it flows through us in the context of a relationship?

At first glance, which of the 5 Essentials most resonates with you? Why?

Which of the 5 Essentials do you think you can most easily incorporate into your daily activities?

SESSION 3 | THE 5 ESSENTIALS + LOVE

Group Discussion

Observe Together

- Share how you have been practicing your "I will" statement.
- Pick a Think It Through question from this session to reflect on with the group.

Read and Process Scripture

Read each verse. Circle one that connects with, encourages, or convicts you.

> Beloved, if God so loved us, we also ought to love one another.
> No one has ever seen God; if we love one another,
> God remains in us, and His love is perfected in us.
>
> —1 JOHN 4:11–12, NASB

> You are from God, little children, and have overcome them; because greater is He who is in you than he who is in the world.
>
> —1 JOHN 4:4, NASB

> But now faith, hope, and love remain, these three;
> but the greatest of these is love.
>
> —1 CORINTHIANS 13:13, NASB

> "You shall love your neighbor as yourself."
>
> —MATTHEW 22:39, NASB

> "This is My commandment, that you love one another,
> just as I have loved you."
>
> —JOHN 15:12, NASB

Which verse did you pick? Contemplate the verse by considering these questions.

What does this verse make you think or feel? Why?

What does this verse tell you about God?

What does this verse tell you about you and your relationship with God?

What do you think the Holy Spirit is prompting you to think about or do differently this week?

Your "I Will" Statement

Based on this session, write an "I will" statement.

I will…

_____

_____

_____

Next Steps

- ○ Pair up with someone in the group and share your "I will" statement.
- ○ Activate your "I will" statement this week.
- ○ Come ready to share how you acted on it next session.
- ○ Bring a friend next week.
- ○ Hear more inspiring stories and practical encouragement on The Blue Cord, by iHOPE Ministries podcast. Find it wherever you listen to podcasts.

Closing Prayer

Journal a short prayer for your week ahead.

SESSION 4

LOOK FOR A PERSON OF PEACE

> **WATCH THE VIDEO: LOOK FOR A PERSON OF PEACE**

Reflect on what you just heard.

What stood out to you from the video?

_____
_____
_____
_____

What challenged or relieved you?

_____
_____
_____
_____

What felt hopeful or freeing?

_____
_____
_____
_____

Session Overview

In John 15, Jesus reminds us that **apart from him, we can do nothing.**

No matter how hard we work to befriend people . . .

No matter how often we invite someone to church . . .

No matter how carefully we explain or reason with someone . . .

Our efforts to share Christ will not bear fruit if we are not working *in partnership with God.*

In the previous session, we saw that this partnership begins with Essential 1: Love—the love of Jesus flowing through us to others. In this session, we'll continue to rely on that divine partnership as we learn to practice **Essential 2: Look for a Person of Peace**—someone God is already wooing to Jesus.

The 5 Essentials

1.	2.	3.	4.	5.
Love in words, actions, and deeds.	**Look for a person of peace.**	Pray together, in Jesus' name.	Share the gospel, early and often.	Share the Bible.

Who Is a Person of Peace?

FORM conversation starters (from Session 2) can help you discern—often quickly—whether you are speaking with a *person of peace*.

You'll know you've encountered a person of peace when he or she responds to your salty speech (spiritual hook) with *curiosity, openness, or eagerness* rather than resistance or indifference.

When Jesus sent out the twelve (Matthew 10) and later the seventy-two (Luke 10), he gave them similar instructions:

SESSION 4 | LOOK FOR A PERSON OF PEACE

> "Whenever you enter someone's home, first say, 'May God's peace be on this house.' If those who live there are peaceful, the blessing will stand; if they are not, the blessing will return to you."
>
> —LUKE 10:5–6, NLT
>
> "As you go into the house, give it your greeting… If the house is worthy, let your peace come upon it; but if it is not worthy, take back your peace."
>
> —MATTHEW 10:12–13, AMP

Jesus knew not everyone would be receptive. His instruction was clear: *stay with the people of peace—and move on when peace is not present.*

God the Father: The One Who Draws

Part of making the most of every opportunity (Colossians 4:6) is learning to recognize the people in whose hearts *God is already at work.*

Read John 6:44–45, 65. Who does Jesus say can come to him?

_____

_____

How does this truth put your role as an ambassador for Christ into perspective?

_____

_____

Jesus was perfect. He taught flawlessly. He healed miraculously. He fed thousands. And still—people rejected him.

We cannot draw people to Jesus. *We don't have that power.* Only God the Father draws people to himself.

What is your role in this divine partnership?

_____
_____
_____
_____

> **STORY: THE SMITHS AND TARA**
>
> Liam and Emma Smith loved people deeply. They were well-educated, culturally aware, and generous with their time. They helped immigrants, international students, and refugees adjust to life in their new community. They loved faithfully—yet fruit was limited.
>
> Eventually, they encountered the ETHNOS course. Learning Essential #2 changed everything.
>
> They realized: *their love, their knowledge, and their effort could not draw people to Jesus.* Only God could do that.
>
> They began praying specifically that God would lead them to **a person of peace**.
>
> Soon after, they met **Tara**, a Buddhist international student.
>
> Emma invited her to a meal and identified herself as a follower of Jesus from the beginning. Tara accepted.
>
> During the meal, conversation turned personal. Tara commented that Liam seemed like a loving father. Liam shared that his ability to be a loving father came from knowing God as his loving heavenly Father. This concept was entirely new—and deeply intriguing—to Tara.
>
> When Liam offered to show Tara what the Bible says about God as Father, she eagerly agreed.
>
> Tara read 1 John 3 and 4 on Liam's phone. She asked thoughtful questions. She wanted to understand more.
>
> The Smiths wondered: *Is God the Father drawing Tara to Jesus?*

The Holy Spirit: The One Who Reveals

Tara was especially curious about references to the Spirit.

The Smiths searched Scripture again and landed on passages about The Holy Spirit's role in revealing truth.

Read the following verses:

- John 14:25
- 1 Corinthians 2:10–14; 12:3
- 1 John 2:27

Based on these scriptures, summarize the Holy Spirit's role with a person of peace.

> No one can say, "Jesus is Lord," except by the Holy Spirit.
> —1 CORINTHIANS 12:3B, NIV

The Holy Spirit removes blindness, reveals truth, and enables understanding. The Spirit was clearly at work in Tara.

The Son: The One Who Receives

> "All those the Father gives me will come to me, and whoever comes to me I will never drive away."
> —JOHN 6:37–39, NIV

> "For my Father's will is that everyone who looks to the Son and believes in him shall have eternal life."
> —JOHN 6:40, NIV

Salvation rests entirely on God's work:

- The **Father** draws
- The **Holy Spirit** reveals
- The **Son** receives

No part of salvation depends on your expertise or perfect words.

Tara eventually placed her faith in Jesus. It took time. It took relationship. And God did the work through the Smiths.

Where Do You Fit In?

Like the Smiths, you may have hesitated because you want to say everything correctly—so you don't mess anything up.

But the truth is freeing: *you don't have to be enough*.

God is enough.

Your role is simpler than you imagine:

- Partner with God.
- Look for people he is already drawing.
- Stay with people of peace.

Read 2 Timothy 4:1–5. What sense of urgency does Paul convey?

_____
_____
_____
_____

What does Paul instruct Timothy to do in verse 2—and when?

_____
_____
_____
_____

What warning does Paul give in verses 3–4?

_____
_____
_____
_____

How has God been preparing you for your role?

Think It Through

What clues have you noticed that suggest you may be engaging a person of peace?

How could practicing this Essential give you more courage to identify as a Jesus-follower?

What do you sense the Holy Spirit prompting you to think about or do differently?

Group Discussion

Observe Together

- Share how you have been practicing your "I will" statement.
- Pick a Think It Through question from this session to reflect on with the group.

Read and Process Scripture

Read the following verses and circle one that connects with, encourages, or convicts you.

> "No one can come to Me unless the Father who sent Me draws him; and I will raise him up on the last day."
>
> —JOHN 6:44, NASB

> And He was saying, "For this reason I have told you that no one can come to Me unless it has been granted him from the Father."
>
> —JOHN 6:65, NASB

> No one can say, "Jesus is Lord," except by the Holy Spirit.
>
> —1 CORINTHIANS 12:3, NASB

> A woman named Lydia was listening. . . . The Lord opened her heart to respond to the things spoken by Paul.
>
> —ACTS 16:14, NASB

> Now after this the Lord appointed seventy-two others, and sent them in pairs ahead of him to every city and place where He Himself was going to come. . . . "And if a man of peace is there, your peace will rest upon him; but if not, it will return to you."
>
> —LUKE 10:1, 6, NASB

Which verse did you pick? Contemplate the verse by considering these questions.

SESSION 4 | LOOK FOR A PERSON OF PEACE

What does this verse make you think or feel? Why?

What does this verse tell you about God?

What does this verse tell you about you and your relationship with God?

What do you think the Holy Spirit is prompting you to do differently this week?

Your "I Will" Statement

Based on this session, write an "I will" statement.

I will…

Next Steps

- ○ Activate your "I will" statement this week.
- ○ Come ready to share how you acted on it next session.
- ○ Bring a friend to the next session.
- ○ Find inspiration to practice what you're learning. Follow iHOPE @iHOPEministries on social media.

Closing Prayer

Journal a short prayer for your week ahead.

SESSION 5

PRAY TOGETHER, IN JESUS' NAME

> **WATCH THE VIDEO: PRAY TOGETHER, IN JESUS' NAME**

Reflect on what you heard in the video.

What stood out to you from the video?

What challenged or relieved you?

What felt hopeful or freeing?

Session Overview

Prayer was a regular part of Jesus' life on earth.

- He went to secluded places to pray often.
- He acknowledged God in prayers of thanksgiving at meals with his followers.
- He prayed for God's miraculous resurrection of his friend Lazarus.
- He prayed for his followers—and for you.
- He prayed in the garden in the hours before he faced the cross.

In **Hebrews 7:25**, we read that Jesus lives to intercede on behalf of all who believe in him as Lord and Savior.

How do you feel knowing that Jesus intercedes on your behalf?

_____
_____
_____

In **Matthew 6**, we see Jesus teaching His followers to pray—even after telling them that God knows what we need before we ask.

If God knows what we need, why does he want us to pray?

_____
_____
_____

The 5 Essentials

1.	2.	3.	4.	5.
Love in words, actions, and deeds.	Look for a person of peace.	**Pray together, in Jesus' name.**	Share the gospel, early and often.	Share the Bible

In this session we focus on **Essential 3: Prayer**—specifically **praying with our other-faith friends in Jesus' name.**

This is a powerful practice for two reasons:

1. It helps you identify whether someone is a *person of peace* (someone God is wooing to Jesus).

When someone accepts your offer to pray with them in Jesus' name, they may be someone God is wooing to Jesus.

2. It is a simple and effective way to *plant a gospel seed*.

Praying with others in Jesus' name is an invitation for God to make himself known in your life and in the life of the person with whom you're praying.

All major religions incorporate prayer. As you learn about how other religions pray—and why—your confidence will grow in why praying in Jesus' name is so distinct and so powerful.

Pray Together Before You Begin

Before we look at how other religions pray, we encourage you to pray now.

As you study other religions, their gods, and the way people pray and worship, take a moment to recognize the reality of the spiritual realm and forces that may be at work behind these false gods. With that reality in mind, bathe this session in prayer.

Pray this prayer aloud yourself or with your group:

Lord, we thank you for this opportunity to be equipped to point people to you. We know there is only one God and only one way to be reconciled to God, and that's through our Lord and Savior Jesus Christ. So, Lord, as we look at these other religions to better understand how to approach people from other faiths with the gospel, we ask for your protection over the minds and hearts of all who take part in this session. May our eyes be focused on you, the one true God. We ask all these things in Jesus's name. Amen.

Understanding Prayer in Other Religions

Prayer is widely practiced across cultures and faiths. You may want to refer back to Session 1: *Understanding World Religions* as you look at each religion's prayer beliefs and customs below.

Prayer Customs	Buddhists	Hindu	Muslims
Frequency	Buddhists pray often, but there is no set time or frequency.	There is no set time or frequency for prayer in Hinduism. Around 70 percent of Hindus pray once daily.	Muslims pray at least five times daily. Prayers are usually before sunrise, at midday, in the late afternoon, at sunset, and at night.
Location	Buddhists pray at a temple with a monk. Being at the temple isn't required for prayer. Buddhists offer incense as part of their prayer ritual.	Hindus pray at temple. They also pray to idols in shrines at home.	Muslims can pray wherever they are. However, many Muslims believe they earn more points (spiritual merit) for praying in the mosque, so they try to pray in there as often as possible.
Length	The typical Buddhist prayer is one hour.	About five minutes.	Prayers are usually five to ten minutes, but they vary.
Why	Buddhists do not pray to a personal god, rather they pray to commune with the divine oneness to which they aspire. They use devotional meditations as prayer with the goals of radiating loving kindness and growing into enlightenment.	Prayers and ceremonial worship in Hinduism is called **puja**. The goal of prayer is to please the gods, grow in enlightenment, and eventually, through the process of reincarnation, become deity. Hindus present offerings as they pray in hope of pleasing their gods and gaining their favor.	Prayer is one of the five pillars of Islam, so it is a religious obligation. Many Muslims practice prayer like a ritual to focus minds and hearts on Allah—to try to please him.

Prayer Customs	Buddhists	Hindu	Muslims
Main Prayer	**Namo Amida Buddha** This prayer, translated below, is an homage to Buddha who represents an example of someone to follow. "O blessed one, precious treasury of compassion, bestower of supreme inner peace, you who love all beings without exception, are the source of happiness and goodness and you guide us to the liberating path."	Hinduism has many prayers, and the main prayer is to **Divine Mother**: "Oh Divine Mother, may your pure divine light illuminate all realms (physical, mental, and spiritual) of our being. Please expel any darkness from our hearts and bestow upon us the true knowledge."	These statements are part of the prayer Muslims pray daily in Arabic: "And I am not among those who associate partners with Allah.... Allah, the one. He begets not, nor is he begotten, and there's none like unto Him."
How	The mantra Buddhists chant during prayer is **Om Mani Padme Hum.** Translated literally, this means "praise to the jewel in the lotus."	During prayer, Hindus will ring a bell to drive away evil. They offer water and food to please their gods. They light candles to symbolize the presence of a god.	Muslims must properly prepare to pray for Allah to hear their prayers. Preparation includes ritualistically washing three times. During prayer, Muslims follow a series of postures including bowing and prostrating themselves in submission to Allah.

Why Pray with Non-Christians?

Prayer is part of every major religion, which means it will not be a foreign concept for most people. Praying to a personal God in Jesus' name, however, is different from every other religion. Only Jesus offers an assured hope of eternity and a loving personal relationship with God.

Does God do miracles when you pray in the name of Jesus?

Personally, I (Renod) have been part of thousands of prayers in Jesus' name with people of other faiths. I have witnessed and know of nineteen miracles of healing. Most of the time there were no physical miracles. During my early days of ministry, I used to worry about whether God would answer prayers for miracles with people of other faiths. I wondered how lack of miraculous healings or such prayers that are seemingly not answered will impact their belief in Jesus.

Yet, thousands of these same people accepted Jesus Christ as Lord and Savior. Many said a similar thing to me—that God did do the main miracle. That's a spiritual miracle of opening their minds and hearts to lead them to salvation in Jesus.

So, don't worry about whether God will answer a prayer in Jesus' name with someone of another faith with a physical miracle. God knows best. He sees their hearts and does spiritual miracles that lead to salvation of people of other faiths.

What are some of the reasons why it would be effective for you to initiate prayer in Jesus' name?

_____

_____

_____

_____

_____

Stories from the Field: Praying in Jesus' Name

God works in many ways when we pray with other-faith friends in Jesus' name. Often, his work is quiet and unseen—slowly softening hearts, building trust, and planting seeds that grow over time. Occasionally, God chooses to act in immediate and visible ways. The stories that follow reflect this range of God's activity. They are not formulas or guarantees—but true accounts of what God can do when his people pray with faithfulness and obedience.

A BUDDHIST'S STORY: FAITHFULNESS OVER TIME

Ava had a close relative who married into a Buddhist family. As Ava grew in her love for God, he also began to shape her heart with compassion for Buddhists. Ava longed to point them to Jesus as Lord and Savior—but she doubted whether a Buddhist would ever accept prayer in Jesus' name.

After learning about the 5 Essentials, Ava felt prompted to try.

Ava befriended Hanh, a Buddhist immigrant navigating intense culture shock. Far from home and familiar support systems, Hanh felt increasingly hopeless about building a new life. She continued her Buddhist prayer routines—chanting and meditating—but found no lasting peace or relief.

One day, Ava gently offered to pray with Hanh in Jesus' name.

Hanh thought, *Why not?* She reasoned that perhaps she could grow in knowledge and enlightenment—or at least feel more hopeful. She accepted Ava's offer.

That was two years ago.

Since then, Hanh has regularly welcomed Ava's prayers in Jesus' name. She often attends church and Bible study with Ava. Over time, Hanh has experienced increasing peace, joy, love, and hope. She understands the gospel clearly, yet has not accepted Jesus as Lord and Savior.

Still, Hanh is a person of peace.

Ava—and others—continue to pray faithfully for her salvation, trusting God's timing and work.

This story reminds us that *praying in Jesus' name is not a technique to force a decision*. It is an invitation for God to work—often patiently, quietly, and over time.

A HINDU'S STORY: FROM RITUAL TO RELATIONSHIP

I grew up in a family of nonbelievers. When I was fourteen, our family doctor introduced me to yoga. While my friends were experimenting with drugs and partying, I immersed myself in yoga, Hindu scriptures, and lectures by Swamis from the Himalayas. Hinduism became my way of life.

Eventually, I began studying to become a Hindu priest. I traveled to India for an arranged marriage. For more than twenty-five years, I practiced Sanskrit prayers and rituals, striving to earn the gods' favor. I was told that enlightenment—becoming one with God—might take many lifetimes.

Instead, I felt increasingly empty.

One day, while lifting weights at my apartment gym, I struck up a conversation with an older man named Robert. He was in his late seventies. We joked about how broken the world seemed. Then, without hesitation, he asked, "Would you want to go to a Bible study with me?"

I had no social life and was hungry for connection, so I said yes.

The next morning, Robert picked me up early. Before we drove off, he prayed in Jesus' name—casually, conversationally, as if God were truly listening. I had never heard anything like it. My prayers had always been formulaic, transactional. This was different.

A few days later, overwhelmed by years of spiritual striving and pain, I stopped doing my mantras. One morning, for the first time in my life, I prayed: *Jesus, please help me.*

That simple prayer changed everything.

I went straight to Robert's house, crying, desperate to understand more about Jesus and the Bible. I became a follower of Christ, and the weight I had carried for decades lifted.

Two weeks later, as I read the Bible one morning, I told my wife, "I think this is true. I think what I've been practicing is wrong." She saw the transformation in me. About a year later, she discarded her Hindu idols and asked me to baptize her as a fellow believer in Christ.

—Jeremy

What Jeremy didn't know was that Robert had recently attended an iHOPE workshop. Robert didn't understand Hinduism. He wasn't an expert. But he practiced the 5 Essentials faithfully—loving well, praying boldly, and trusting God with the outcome.

Robert walked with Jeremy for nearly three years before Jeremy accepted Christ. His obedience—and God's Word—did the work.

A MUSLIM'S STORY: WHEN GOD ACTS POWERFULLY

Kari knew that Islam denies the crucifixion and the deity of Jesus. Before taking ETHNOS, she wondered, *How could a Muslim ever accept prayer in Jesus' name?*

After learning about the 5 Essentials, Kari created her "I Will" statement and committed to act. She volunteers as a language conversation partner with international students at a local university—giving her regular opportunities to practice what she was learning.

One day, Kari noticed a young woman sitting alone at lunch, visibly distressed. Kari struck up a conversation, and within minutes the student—Dalilah—burst into tears.

Dalilah shared that she was a devout Muslim from an Islamic country. As a child, her parents believed she was demon-possessed. Later, she was diagnosed with clinical depression and endured years of medication and severe side effects. She suffered from recurring suicidal thoughts.

Dalilah and her parents prayed persistently at the mosque—sometimes up to twelve times a day—but she found no healing.

Now alone in a new country, separated from her support system, Dalilah felt overwhelmed.

As Kari listened, she sensed the Holy Spirit prompting her to pray. She felt nervous, but remembered what she had learned in ETHNOS—that prayer in Jesus' name is both loving and revealing. She decided to trust God with the outcome.

Kari gently offered to pray for Dalilah in Jesus' name, explaining, "I pray in Jesus' name because Jesus is at the right hand of God, interceding for us."

Dalilah thought, *Why not?* Another prayer—even from a Christian—couldn't hurt.

They closed their eyes, and Kari prayed.

When the prayer ended, Dalilah sat silently. Then she smiled. The smile turned into laughter. She stood up, laughing and jumping, overwhelmed by a joy she had never experienced before.

Dalilah later explained that when Kari said, *"In Jesus' name,"* she saw what looked like the hand of God gently removing a heavy, dark heart from within her—and replacing it with a new, bright, healthy one. In that moment, the sadness lifted. Joy flooded in.

Jesus was the difference.

God used Kari to lead Dalilah to Christ as Lord and Savior.

Important note: Most prayers in Jesus' name do not result in immediate, visible transformation. But every prayer invites the presence and authority of Christ into a person's life. Our role is faithfulness. God determines the outcome.

Steps for Initiating Prayer in Jesus' Name

1. Be purposeful.

Pray and watch for divine appointments with persons of peace.

2. Embrace crucial moments.

Decide ahead of time that you will push past awkwardness to initiate prayer in Jesus' name.

3. Know your words.

Knowing what you will say prepares you to confidently lean into the moment.

The video offered an example of what to say when the Holy Spirit nudges you to pray with someone:

> God must really love you. He nudged me just now to say hello and to pray for you. My name is _____. Is there something I can pray for you right now?

Write out words you could use to initiate prayer with someone.

_____
_____
_____
_____
_____

4. Identify yourself as a Jesus-follower and ask for permission to pray in Jesus' name.

Explain what you are going to do and why. As a Christian, you will end the prayer by appealing to God in the name of Jesus.

Sample Words to Say

> I pray in Jesus' name because God revealed in the Holy Bible in Romans 8:34, that Jesus is at the right hand of God and is interceding for us. How may I pray for you right now?

> I pray in the name of Jesus because of what God revealed about Jesus in Hebrews 7:25: "Therefore he is able to save completely those who come to God through Him because He always lives to intercede for them." How may I pray for you right now?

5. Pray together, in Jesus' name.

Before you pray, pause and silently ask the Holy Spirit to guide your words. Then, pray for the person and end your prayer with the words, *in Jesus' name, amen.*

Practice This Essential Everywhere

Follow the Holy Spirit's direction. Prayer is legal most everywhere and used in all religions!

Just as Jesus intercedes for us, God's Holy Spirit prays for us. Romans 8:26–27 says the Spirit lifts up requests on our behalf when we don't know what to ask for or how to pray.

If Someone Objects or Doesn't Understand

In this session's video, Renod shares this simple script:

> My friend, I understand this can be difficult. This is what God reveals in the Holy Bible: "The person without the Spirit does not accept the things that come from the Spirit of God but considers them foolishness and cannot understand them because they are discerned only through the Spirit." This verse from 1 Corinthians 2:14 simply says that people need the Spirit to understand spiritual things.

Prayer is widely practiced across cultures and faiths because every faith believes in a spiritual being, this verse and a prayer asking for God's Holy Spirit to reveal truth is both inoffensive and exceptionally powerful.

Sample Prayer

Holy Spirit of God, please reveal, guide, and teach us the truth as we study God's word together. In Jesus' name. Amen.

Think It Through

How does prayer from other major world religions contrast with Christian prayer?

What are some of the reasons why it would be effective for you to initiate prayer in Jesus' name?

_____
_____
_____

Of the steps for initiating prayer, which one(s) are you most comfortable practicing?

_____
_____
_____

Which steps do you need to get more comfortable with?

_____
_____
_____

What would stand in the way of you practicing the steps to initiate prayer?

_____
_____
_____

Group Discussion

Observe Together

- Share how you have been practicing your "I will" statement.
- Pick a Think It Through question from this session to reflect on with the group.

Read and Process Scripture

Read the following verses. Circle one that connects with, encourages, or convicts you. Contemplate the scripture for a few moments.

> Who is the one who condemns? Christ Jesus is He who died, but rather, was raised, who is at the right hand of God, who also intercedes for us.
>
> —ROMANS 8:34, NASB
>
> Therefore He is also able to save forever those who come to God through Him, since He always lives to make intercession for them.
>
> —HEBREWS 7:25, NASB
>
> For there is one God, and one mediator also between God and mankind, the man Christ Jesus, who gave Himself as a ransom for all, the testimony given at the proper time.
>
> —1 TIMOTHY 2:5–6, NASB
>
> For Christ did not enter a holy place made by hands, a mere copy of the true one, but into heaven itself, now to appear in the presence of God for us.
>
> —HEBREWS 9:24, NASB

Which verse did you pick? Contemplate the verse by considering these questions.

What does this verse make you think or feel? Why?

_____
_____
_____

What does this verse tell you about God?

_____
_____
_____

What does this verse tell you about you and your relationship with God?

_____
_____
_____

What do you think the Holy Spirit is prompting you to think about or do differently this week?

_____
_____
_____

Your "I Will" Statement

Based on this session, write an "I will" statement that you want to focus on this week.

I will . . .

_____
_____
_____

Pair up with someone in the group and share your "I will" statement.

Next Steps

- ○ Activate your "I will" statement this week.
- ○ Come ready to share how you activated your "I will" statement at the next session.
- ○ With your small group, or with a friend, take a field trip to meet people from other faiths—like an ethnic festival, market, or restaurant. Pray with expectation, and practice some of the ETHNOS concepts you have been learning.
- ○ Listen to a Blue Cord, by iHOPE Ministries' podcast at iHOPEministries.org.

Closing Prayer

Journal a short prayer for your week ahead.

SESSION 6

SHARE THE GOSPEL, EARLY AND OFTEN

> **WATCH THE VIDEO: SHARE THE GOSPEL, EARLY AND OFTEN**

Take a moment to reflect on what you just heard.

How many times do other-faith friends typically need to hear the gospel before they accept Christ?

How long does it take for someone to accept Jesus as Lord and Savior?

Why does it take so long? (Look back at the chart on page 26 from Session 1, Understanding World Religions, as you think through your answer.)

Session Overview

In this session, you'll explore **Essential 5: Share the gospel, early and often.**

Sharing the gospel is not "extra credit" for a few gifted evangelists. It's part of what it means to love people—because the gospel is the only message that offers *forgiveness, reconciliation with God, and eternal life through Jesus.*

The good news is that sharing the gospel doesn't need to be complicated. You don't have to be a Bible expert or theologian. You don't need a long, drawn-out explanation. You can plant a gospel seed in just a few seconds—simply by sharing what you believe about Jesus.

> "Go into all the world and preach the gospel to all creation."
> —MARK 16:15–16, CSB

The 5 Essentials

1. Love in words, actions, and deeds	2. Look for a person of peace.	3. Pray together, in Jesus' name.	**4. Share the gospel, early and often.**	5. Share the Bible.

No More Bad Evangelism

Have you ever sat through a hell-fire-and-brimstone sermon? Or maybe you've seen someone standing on a busy street carrying a sign, like "The wages of sin is death!"

Even if you are a believer and know Romans 6:23 by heart, fear tactics and evangelism that relies on intimidation don't feel like love. That kind of evangelism seems like a personal attack. It can even feel like hate.

SESSION 6 | SHARE THE GOSPEL, EARLY AND OFTEN

Have you observed or experienced "bad evangelism?" How has it impacted your Christian witness?

STORY: TAYLOR LEARNS TO SHARE THE GOSPEL

Taylor took ETHNOS at her church. For years, she had coworkers and neighbors from other faiths—but she kept her faith in Jesus to herself. She was afraid of offending them.

In the past, Taylor had studied evangelism materials and learned several gospel methods. But she wasn't sure which—if any—were appropriate with people from other faiths. She couldn't imagine herself using them. So, despite her sincere faith, Taylor admitted that she had never shared the gospel with someone from another culture or religion.

As the ETHNOS Course progressed, something shifted. Taylor realized she didn't need a polished presentation or expert knowledge. She needed clarity, courage, and simple obedience. Week by week, her confidence grew.

After this session, Taylor wrote a short, simple gospel message in her own words. In her "I Will" statement, she committed to share the gospel with her Hindu neighbor.

By the eighth and final session of ETHNOS, Taylor shared that she had followed through. Not only had she shared the gospel with her Hindu neighbor—she had also shared it with a Buddhist and a Muslim.

ETHNOS didn't turn Taylor into an evangelism expert. It helped remove her fear, gave her words she could actually use, and ignited her to boldly share Jesus with people of other faiths and cultures.

The One-Sentence Gospel

As Taylor discovered, the good news about the Good News is that you don't have to know everything. Nor do you need to do everything perfectly. Sharing the gospel can be done simply in one sentence.

Verses, like Romans 10:9, are a great way to explain what you believe in a simple, concise way.

Here are the words Taylor wrote to share a two-sentence gospel presentation, using Romans 10:9:

I'm a follower of Jesus. That means that I believe what God reveals in the Holy Bible, that "if you confess with your mouth that Jesus is Lord and believe in your heart that God raised him from the dead, you'll be saved." How about you? What do you believe?

Taylor began to be purposeful about sharing the gospel like that as soon as appropriate in a new relationship with someone from another faith.

Write a short paragraph gospel using Romans 10:9 or another easy-to-remember verse and your own words.

_____
_____
_____
_____
_____

It Takes Time

Do you remember the first time you heard the gospel? If you grew up going to a Christian church, chances are good that you heard the gospel many times over many years before you accepted Jesus as your personal Lord and Savior. The same will be true for friends of other faiths.

Patience and persistence are virtues to practice when you're sharing Jesus with your other-faith friends. It is rare for someone—even a person of peace—to accept Jesus as Lord and Savior the very first time they hear the gospel.

Here's why: Non-Christian religions are based on works and on trying to earn salvation or reach a state of divinity. Refer to the Understanding World Religions Chart in Session 1 to complete the following sentences.

Muslims believe Jesus was _____.

Hindus believe Jesus was _____.

Buddhists believe Jesus was _____.

People who hold to secular and various spiritual teachings believe Jesus was _____ .

Facts to Remember

Read Ephesians 2:8–9 (NASB) and complete the scripture:

For by _____ you have been saved through _____; and this is not of yourselves, it is the _____ of God; not as a result of _____, so that no one may boast.

Read John 14:6 (NASB) and complete the scripture:

Jesus said to him, "I am the _____, and the _____, and the _____; no one comes to the Father except through _____."

Steps to Sharing the Gospel Early and Often

The steps you used to initiate prayer with someone in Jesus' name are the same steps you use to share the gospel.

1. Be an intentional, authentic witness.

Prepare your heart and mind by reading God's Word and praying for and expecting divine appointments.

2. Embrace crucial moments.

Decide in advance that you will respond when the Holy Spirit nudges you to share the gospel with someone.

3. Know your words.

Memorizing Romans 10:9 now can help boost your confidence when a crucial moment comes. Be genuine and remember that you are sharing something that points to Jesus.

4. Identify with Jesus early and always.

If people know nothing else about you, they should know that you follow Christ, and what that means.

> "As you go, proclaim this message: 'The kingdom of heaven has come near.' . . . Freely you have received; freely give."
>
> —MATTHEW 10:7–8, NIV

Early and Often

Notice the words early and often in Essential 4. Sharing the gospel with people is easier when you bring Jesus into the relationship early.

One of the biggest mistakes Christians make is building relationships on everything but Christ to be culturally correct. The longer you wait, the more awkward sharing your faith will become. Here's why: If your faith in God and relationship with Jesus is important to you, your friend of another faith expects you to bring it up. Neglecting to do so signals that your Christian faith isn't important to you. Delaying to mention your faith diminishes your witness. You want your other-faith friends to realize that you and Jesus are a "package deal." Think: You want to be friends with me? You're going to get Jesus too.

But what if you've befriended someone from another faith and have a great relationship with that person but have never talked about Jesus?

Start fresh. Being an effective witness means being authentic, so just own up to it. The sample scripts that follow provide you with an easy way to bring Jesus into your relationships.

Sample Words to Say

> There's something I've been wanting to tell you for a while now. I'm a follower of Jesus. That just means that I believe that if you confess with your mouth that Jesus is Lord and believe in your heart that God raised him from

the dead, you'll be saved. My faith is important to me, and I should have told you before now. How do you feel about that?

Here's another:

We've talked about a lot of things but never faith. I don't know why I've held back from sharing that I'm a follower of Jesus. My faith is really important to me. Has anyone ever shared with you what followers of Jesus believe?

Do you have friends with whom you haven't talked about your faith? If so, write down their names and what you could say to them about your faith the next time you talk.

_____

_____

_____

Don't assume that people know you are a follower of Jesus or that they know what it that means to be a follower of Jesus. If your faith is important to you, share it.

SARAH'S STORY

I was trying hard to be a good Buddhist girl. I studied hard to get good grades, did all my Buddhist chants, tried to obey Buddha's teachings. But somehow it was never enough for my aunt. She was constantly berating me. "Your mom is a fool. Your dad is dead. It's better that you die."

Her words hurt me deeply. I internalized her words and seriously wondered "If I die now, I might go to hell. Or I'll be reincarnated as a cat or a monkey." I didn't think I was good enough to be reincarnated as a human.

I shared the whole awful situation with my English teacher. I didn't know she was a believer. She encouraged me, "You are not bad. You are nice." Then she invited me to church. Her invitation intrigued me. I had never thought about visiting a church. I thought it was only for Westerners, not people like me.

Curious, I went with her. I remember seeing lots of people singing. A man got up on the stage, opened a big book, and talked about God, creation, sin, separation from God, and salvation. I'd never heard this story before, and I know he was reading from the Bible.

The gospel message caught my attention. I didn't understand it all, but I kept going back to church to learn more. Then I began studying the Bible too. In time, I began to realize that I was a sinner. I repented and accepted Jesus as my Lord and Savior. On the day it happened, God seemed to speak directly to me through the Bible, "Don't be discouraged. Don't worry about the future. Even though you don't have a Father on earth, you have a Father in heaven."

Now I know that God is real. He loves me and is taking care of me. I am not going to be a monkey or a cat when I die. Now my eternal destiny is secure. This fills me with awe and makes me strong.

—Sarah

Think It Through

Have you observed or experienced "bad evangelism?" How has it impacted your Christian witness?

_____
_____
_____

What burdens have you placed on yourself around sharing the gospel?

_____
_____
_____

How is the Lord stirring you to think or act differently regarding the way you share your faith?

_____
_____
_____

What would hold you back from identifying yourself as a follower of Jesus and explaining what that means early in a relationship?

_____
_____
_____
_____

What small steps (such as memorizing Romans 10:9) will you take to develop your confidence to share the gospel more freely?

_____

_____

_____

Are you willing to put yourself out there and share a simple one-sentence statement like Romans 10:9 with someone of another faith? Why or why not?

_____

_____

_____

Group Discussion

Observe Together

- Share how you have been practicing your "I will" statement.
- Pick a Think It Through question from this session to reflect on with the group.

Read and Process Scripture

Read each of the following verses. Circle one that connects with, encourages, or convicts you. Contemplate the scripture for a few moments.

> "And I will make you into a great nation, and I will bless you, and make your name great; and you shall be a blessing."
>
> —GENESIS 12:2, NASB

> Proclaim the good news of His salvation from day to day. Tell of His glory among the nations, His wonderful deeds among all the peoples.
>
> —PSALM 96:2–3, NASB

> Namely, that God was in Christ reconciling the world to Himself, not counting their wrongdoings against them, and He has committed to us the word of reconciliation. Therefore, we are ambassadors for Christ, as though God were making an appeal through us; we beg you on behalf of Christ, be reconciled to God.
>
> —2 CORINTHIANS 5:19–20, NASB

Which verse did you pick? Contemplate the verse by considering these questions.

What does this verse make you think or feel? Why?

What does this verse tell you about God?

What does this verse tell you about you and your relationship with God?

What do you think the Holy Spirit is prompting you to think about or do differently this week?

SESSION 6 | SHARE THE GOSPEL, EARLY AND OFTEN

Your "I Will" Statement

Based on this session, write an "I will" statement that you want to focus on this week.

I will . . .

Next Steps

- ○ Tell someone what your "I will" statement is. Invite them to check in with you to see how you are activating it this week.
- ○ Come ready to share how you activated your "I will" statement at the next session.
- ○ Pray about leading others through this ETHNOS study. How might you pay this experience forward?

Closing Prayer

Journal a short prayer for your week ahead.

SESSION 7

SHARE THE BIBLE

WATCH THE VIDEO: SHARE THE BIBLE

As you watch, listen for three simple themes:

- You don't need to defend the Bible.
- You can trust God's Word to speak for itself
- God's Word + God's Spirit does what you cannot.

Take a moment to reflect on what you just heard.

What stood out to you?

What felt freeing?

What challenged you?

_____
_____
_____

Session Overview

You've made it to the final session of ETHNOS. Over the past eight sessions, you've been equipped to live as an authentic witness—someone who loves well, looks for people of peace, prays in Jesus' name, and shares the gospel naturally.

When you practice the 5 Essentials in your daily life, you allow God to work through your love, your words and prayers, and the gospel seeds you plant. All of these work together to point people toward a personal, loving, eternal relationship with God through Jesus.

But there is one more seed to plant—one that is more powerful and effective than anything you can say on your own: *God's Word*.

In this final session, we focus on **Essential 5: Share the Bible.** When you share God's Word with a person of peace, you are placing something in their hands that is more powerful than anything you can do or say—because the Holy Spirit uses Scripture to reveal Jesus.

> For the word of God is living and active and sharper than any two-edged sword, and piercing as far as the division of soul and spirit, of both joints and marrow, and able to judge the thoughts and intentions of the heart.
>
> —HEBREWS 4:12, NASB

Essential 5 is to share the Bible with people. When you give a Bible to a person of peace, the Holy Spirit reveals the truth of Jesus each time that person reads or listens to God's Word.

The 5 Essentials

1.	2.	3.	4.	5.
Love in words, actions, and deeds.	Look for a person of peace.	Pray together, in Jesus' name.	Share the gospel, early and often.	**Share the Bible.**

In this session, you will explore why sharing the Bible with someone from another faith is so effective—and how simple it can be. You will also learn what makes the Bible unique among the scriptures of other world religions.

Why Sharing the Bible Is So Effective

As an authentic Christian witness, you look for people whom God is drawing to himself—persons of peace. One way you discern this is by sharing the Bible.

Not everyone will be interested. That's okay.

Continue loving them. Keep practicing the other Essentials. Do not take their disinterest personally. They may not be a person of peace—*yet*.

What clues might you notice that would prompt you to share the Bible with a nonbeliever?

_____

_____

_____

_____

_____

_____

_____

The Bible for Every Nation

The purpose of this course is to equip believers like you to boldly reveal Christ with people from every tribe and people and language. When you give someone a Bible in their own language, you make it easier for them to encounter Jesus.

> **TIP**
> The YouVersion Bible app offers Scripture in more than 2,000 languages and is available on most devices.

Technology makes this more accessible than ever. With Bible apps that offer Scripture in thousands of languages and dialects, people can read or listen to God's Word right on their phones.

Sometimes all it takes is a simple question: *Has anyone ever given you a Bible?*

How could practicing this Essential empower you?

_____

_____

_____

What's so Special about the Bible?

Every major world religion has written scriptures or sacred writings. The chart that follows highlights what makes the Bible unique.

Key Points to Note

- God revealed His word through more than forty prophets.
- God's inspired word was revealed, written, and collected over 1,500 years.
- All of Scripture points to Jesus—the one who redeems humanity and restores relationship with our loving creator.

The Bible contains multiple genres, including poetry that reveals the character of God and humanity's relationship with him; 1,400 years of historical prophecies as well as future prophecies; 4,000 years of historical events that are recorded and verified by archeology and science.

What Makes the Holy Scriptures Different?

Topic	Christianity	Islam	Hinduism	Buddhism	Spiritual
Holy Scripture	Bible	Quran	Vedas	Tripitaka	Impersonal divine oneness
Source Origin	God Written	Allah Oral	Gods Oral	Buddha Oral	Many Oral
Human Source	40 Prophets	Muhammad	Many	Many	Many
Revelation Period	1,400 BC–100 AD	600–620 AD	1,500 BC–Ongoing	400 BC–Ongoing	400 BC–Ongoing
Purpose	Jesus	Allah	Enlightenment	Enlightenment	Enlightenment
Poetry	Yes	Yes	Yes	Yes	Yes
Prophecy Fulfilled/Future	1,400 Years Many	None Judgement Day	None None	None None	None None
History Inaccuracies	4,000 Years None	20 Years Yes	None N/A	None N/A	None N/A
Historical Dates	Many and accurate	Few and inaccurate	None	None	None
Archeological Evidence/Science	Since creation Ahead of human knowledge	20 Years None	None None	None None	None None

A Word about Objections and Misunderstandings

One of the major teachings in Islam is that the Bible has been corrupted. Other religions deny that Jesus is the only way for people to know God. When someone challenges you about the Bible, remember that God's Word defends itself. You do not need to defend the Bible. Let God's Holy Spirit defend and reveal the truths he inspired.

Two Approaches, Two Outcomes

Mohammad—a believer from a Muslim background highlighted in Session One—is a subject matter expert on the Quran and Islamic theology. If anyone could successfully defend the Bible against objections, it would be Mohammad.

Over nine years, Mohammad helped lead about seventy Muslims to faith in Jesus—a faithful harvest.

Most believers do not have Mohammad's background or training. And perhaps you don't either. In fact, you may be more like Joe.

Joe didn't know much about other faiths. But he was filled with the Holy Spirit and trusted the power of God's Word. Joe didn't argue or defend the Bible. He answered honest questions with humility and consistently shared Scripture.

Over the same nine-year period, in the same region, *Joe helped lead around six hundred Muslims to faith in Jesus.*

Joe practiced the 5 Essentials faithfully—especially looking for persons of peace and sharing the Bible freely.

You can do the same.

MATEO'S STORY—AN ORDINARY BELIEVER STEPS FORWARD

Mateo is a store manager who intentionally tithes his time to serve as an ambassador for Christ. He volunteers with international students, refugees, and immigrants, building genuine friendships marked by kindness and hospitality.

For years, Mateo loved people well—but rarely spoke about Jesus. He believed he needed to know more about other faiths and cultures before sharing his faith without offending.

After attending an overview workshop on the 5 Essentials, Mateo realized something surprising: he didn't need expertise. He needed obedience, dependence on the Holy Spirit, and courage to take the next step.

Inspired by Joe's example, Mateo began practicing the 5 Essentials.

Not long after, Mateo met Omar, a Muslim international student—and an Islamic theologian. Omar eagerly discussed spiritual topics, offered Mateo a Quran, and even invited him to a Quran study.

Mateo felt intimidated. Quietly, he prayed for the Holy Spirit's guidance.

In that moment, Mateo sensed a simple prompting:

Offer Omar a Bible.

What happened next reveals the power of sharing God's Word.

Steps to Sharing the Bible

The same steps you've used to pray with someone and share the gospel apply here.

- **Be an intentional witness.** Look for clues that someone may be a person of peace.
- **Embrace crucial moments.** Respond when the Holy Spirit nudges you.
- **Know your words.** Be genuine. You are sharing life-giving truth.
- **Identify with Jesus.** Reading and discussing Scripture is a critical step on the journey to Christ.

OMAR'S STORY—WHEN GOD'S WORD IS UNLEASHED

When Omar offered Mateo a Quran and a study, Mateo smiled and replied, *"Thank you. I'll accept a Quran and study with you—if you'll accept a Holy Bible and study it with me."*

Omar objected. "The Bible has been corrupted."

Mateo calmly shared a few Scriptures with Omar in response.

> **The grass withers, the flower fades, but the word of our God stands forever.**
> —ISAIAH 40:8

> **Heaven and earth will pass away, but My words will not pass away.**
> —MARK 13:31

Then Mateo asked, *"May I give you a Holy Bible so you can examine God's Word for yourself?"*

Omar paused, then said, "Okay."

Omar accepted the Bible—but not without fear.

Alone in his apartment, Omar felt overwhelmed. He dropped the Bible, afraid something powerful was attached to it. For days, it sat hidden in a closet.

Eventually, curiosity overcame fear. Omar opened the New Testament and read the Gospel of Matthew—*in one evening*.

He objected strongly to the crucifixion and resurrection. "That's the corruption," he thought.

Mateo responded not with debate—but with Scripture:

> **No one knows the thoughts of God except the Spirit of God.**
> —1 CORINTHIANS 2:11B, NIV

> **The person without the Spirit does not accept the things that come from the Spirit of God but considers them foolishness, and cannot understand them because they are discerned only through the Spirit.**
> —1 CORINTHIANS 2:14, NIV

> Mateo asked to pray that the Spirit of God will reveal the truth. Omar agreed.
>
> For more than a year, Omar continued reading Scripture. Slowly, the Holy Spirit worked, making Jesus known to him.
>
> Eventually, Omar faced a decision. He knew the Quran and the Bible could not both be true. Accepting Jesus would cost him his family, inheritance, and safety.
>
> Counting the cost, Omar decided Jesus was worth it all.
>
> What began with a simple act—*offering a Bible*—led to transformation, discipleship, and multiplication.

Sample Words to Say

> I know you are feeling anxious about (topic). I've felt that way too. You know I am a follower of Jesus, and reading the Bible gives me a lot of peace when I'm feeling anxious. Would you like to check out what God's Word has to say about (topic)?

When you share God's Word with someone, you are partnering with him. Continue that partnership by praying with and for the person, asking God's Holy Spirit to reveal truth through Scripture. Be available to study the Bible with your other-faith friends, and remember that it is the Holy Spirit that enables them to understand what they're reading.

Commissioning: You Are Now Part of the Story

This course began with a reminder that **a war is waging in the universe**—a battle for truth, allegiance, and worship.

You are not a bystander in that war.

Each time you love across faiths, pray in Jesus' name, share the gospel, or place God's Word into someone's hands, you step onto the front lines—not with arguments but with obedience.

You are not called to win debates.

You are called to *faithful partnership*.

And God does the rest.

Think It Through

What clues might you notice that would prompt you to share the Bible with a nonbeliever?

Have you ever shared the Bible with a nonbeliever? Explain.

How could practicing this Essential empower you?

What would get in the way of you sharing the Bible?

> It is just as the Scripture says: "Anyone who believes in Him will never be put to shame." For there is no difference between Jew and Greek: The same Lord is Lord of all, and gives richly to all who call on Him, for, "Everyone who calls on the name of the Lord will be saved."
>
> How then can they call on the One in whom they have not believed? **And how can they believe in the One of whom they have not heard?** And how can they hear without someone to preach? And how can they preach unless they are sent? As it is written: "How beautiful are the feet of those who bring good news!"
>
> —ROMANS 10:11–15, NIV (EMPHASIS ADDED)

Group Discussion

Observe Together

- Share how you have been practicing your "I will" statement.
- Pick a Think It Through question from this session to reflect on with the group.

Read and Process Scripture

Read each of the following verses. Circle one that connects with, encourages, or convicts you. Contemplate the scripture for a few moments.

> For I am not ashamed of the gospel, for it is the power of God for salvation to everyone who believes, to the Jew first and also to the Greek.
>
> —ROMANS 1:16, NASB

> All Scripture is inspired by God and beneficial for teaching, for rebuke, for correction, for training in righteousness; so that the man or woman of God may be fully capable, equipped for every good work.
>
> —2 TIMOTHY 3:16–17, NASB

> Then He opened their minds to understand the Scriptures.
>
> —LUKE 24:45, NASB

> "Heaven and earth will pass away, but My words will not pass away."
>
> —MARK 13:31, NASB

> "Is My word not like fire?" declares the Lord, "and like a hammer which shatters a rock?"
>
> —JEREMIAH 23:29, NASB.

What does this verse make you think or feel? Why?

What does this verse tell you about God?

What does this verse tell you about you and your relationship with God?

What do you think the Holy Spirit is prompting you to think about or do differently going forward?

Your "I Will" Statement

Based on this session, write an "I will" statement that you want to focus on next.

I will . . .

_____
_____
_____
_____

Practice Living as an Authentic Christian Witness Across Faiths

> After this I looked, and there before me was a great multitude that no one could count, from every nation, tribe, people and language.
>
> —REVELATION 7:9A, NIV

What a beautiful picture of the future! Believers from every tongue, tribe, nation, and language will one day worship God together.

You have the privilege of partnering with God by sharing the hope and freedom that Jesus offers. Now that you have completed ETHNOS, you are ready and equipped to boldly reveal Christ across faiths. Practice what you've learned and boldly live as an authentic witness in your everyday life. There are people all around you who are lost and hurting. They need Jesus as much as you do!

Next Steps

Because this is the final session, your "next steps" matter. The goal isn't simply to finish ETHNOS—*it's to live out the things you've learned.*

1. Activate your "I will" statement going forward.

How will you continue to practice ETHNOS concepts in your daily life?

_____

_____

_____

2. Take the survey again.

Take the same survey you took earlier in the course so you can see—clearly and measurably—**how much you've grown** in your thoughts, fears, confidence, and actions.

3. Keep practicing the 5 Essentials—weekly.

Love. Look. Pray. Share the gospel. Share the Bible. Repeat.

4. Stay connected for ongoing encouragement.

Connect with the greater iHOPE Community. Go to iHOPEministries.org to sign up to receive emails with inspiring stories, upcoming events, and more resources that ignite and equip you to share the hope of Jesus.

5. Pay this experience forward.

Tell others how this course impacted you. Consider taking people in your circle of influence through the study.

A Simple Prayer

Lord, thank you for what you've taught me through ETHNOS. Help me live this out with love, courage, and dependence on you. Show me the next faithful step—and give me the grace to take it.

In Jesus' name, amen.

APPENDIX

YOUR NEXT STEPS AFTER ETHNOS

A Pathway for Living, Practicing, and Multiplying the 5 Essentials

ETHNOS is not the finish line—it's a launch point.

Now that you've completed the ETHNOS Course, you're ignited and equipped to reveal Christ across faiths. But this is not the end of the journey. *It's the beginning of a new way of living as a Spirit-led ambassador for Jesus.*

Transformation happens when what you've learned becomes what you practice.

Multiplication happens when what you practice is passed on to others.

The following steps will help you discern how God may be inviting you to continue.

Step 1: Live It Personally

Practice the 5 Essentials in your everyday life. The first and most important next step is faithful obedience in ordinary moments.

What This Looks Like

- Intentionally loving people from other faiths and cultures

- Looking for persons of peace God is already drawing to himself
- Praying with people in Jesus' name when opportunities arise
- Sharing the gospel naturally—early and often
- Offering Scripture and inviting others to encounter God's Word

Simple Practices

- Pray daily: *"Lord, show me who you are already working in."*
- Reflect weekly on your "I Will" statement from Session 7.
- Keep spiritual conversations relational, not rushed.
- Trust God with outcomes—your role is obedience, not results.

Remember: God does the saving. You get the joy of partnering with him.

Step 2: Practice in Community

Grow through accountability, prayer, and shared learning. Discipleship flourishes in community. Practicing the 5 Essentials alongside others helps sustain courage, humility, and faithfulness.

Ways to Practice Together

- Stay connected with one or two people from your ETHNOS group.
- Share stories of where you've noticed God at work.
- Pray together for specific people of peace.
- Study Scripture together with a gospel lens.
- Encourage one another when conversations feel awkward or slow.

Helpful Question: *Who could I invite to walk this journey with me for the next season?*

Community keeps ETHNOS from becoming a memory instead of a lifestyle.

Step 3: Lead Others Through ETHNOS

Multiply what God has done in you. One of the most powerful ways to grow is to help others experience what you've experienced.

You do *not* need to be:

- an expert in world religions,
- a seasoned evangelist,
- or a gifted teacher.

You simply need to be one step ahead and willing to facilitate, not dominate.

Signs That You Might Be Ready to Facilitate

- You felt personally challenged and encouraged by ETHNOS.
- You are practicing the 5 Essentials imperfectly but faithfully.
- You enjoy drawing others into discussion.
- You are willing to rely on the Holy Spirit, not your own expertise.

Facilitators don't need all the answers—they help people *process, practice,* and *pray.*

ETHNOS grows best when participants become facilitators.

Step 4: Help Create a Culture of Multiplication

Raise the outreach temperature of your church or group. ETHNOS is most fruitful when it becomes part of an organization's discipleship culture, not just a standalone course.

Ways to Multiply Impact

- Encourage your church to offer ETHNOS regularly.
- Invite youth (ages 12 and up) into appropriate ETHNOS groups.
- Share testimonies with church leaders.
- Mentor a new facilitator as they lead their first group.
- Model a humble, Spirit-dependent posture toward outreach.

Imagine a church where sharing Jesus across faiths and cultures is *normal, prayerful, and relational*—not intimidating or rare.

A FINAL WORD OF ENCOURAGEMENT

You will not always say the perfect words, feel confident, or see immediate fruit.

That's okay.

God delights in faithful obedience, not flawless performance.

> *I planted the seed, Apollos watered it, but God has been making it grow.*
> *—1 CORINTHIANS 3:6, NIV*

Continue the Journey with iHOPE Resources

ETHNOS is part of a broader discipleship ecosystem created by **iHOPE Ministries** to help believers ignite their faith and live missionally across faiths and cultures. If this course has stirred your heart to love, pray, and share Jesus more intentionally, we invite you to continue growing through the following iHOPE resources.

The Blue Cord Women's Book Study and Resources

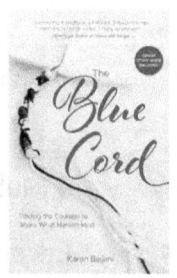

The Blue Cord book study and related resources are designed to help women grow as **courageous, compassionate witnesses of Christ** among people of other faiths and cultures. Rooted in Scripture and real-life stories, The Blue Cord creates space for honest wrestling, prayer, and spiritual growth—helping women move from fear to faithful action.

Blue Cord resources include:

- *The Blue Cord,* a six-week book study for individuals and groups
- **The Blue Cord, by iHOPE Ministries podcast,** which features inspiring real-life stories and conversations about faith, courage, and cross-cultural discipleship

- Conferences, city groups, and leadership pathways for women who want to disciple others

Books for Deeper Engagement with Muslim Seekers

For those who desire to grow specifically in understanding and engaging Muslim friends with clarity and compassion, iHOPE founder Renod Bejjani has authored two practical resources:

Muslims: 5 Biblical Essentials Every Christian Must Know and Do, a clear, accessible guide that equips everyday believers to understand Islam biblically and engage Muslim neighbors with truth, love, and confidence.

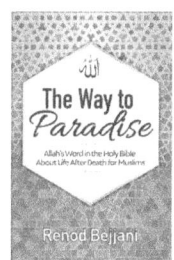

The Way to Paradise: Allah's Word in the Holy Bible about Life after Death for Muslims, an evangelistic Bible study designed for Muslim seekers, guiding readers through Scripture to explore who Jesus is and what it means to follow him.

These resources pair naturally with the ETHNOS Course and are especially helpful for participants who sense God calling them to deeper relationships with Muslim friends, neighbors, classmates, or coworkers locally and globally.

Additional Resources

- ETHNOS Kids resources for younger generations—coming soon
- ETHNOS Experience—immersive cultural experience for the whole family
- ETHNOS Facilitator Training for churches and groups

TO EXPLORE THESE RESOURCES OR LEARN MORE, VISIT IHOPEMINISTRIES.ORG.

ABOUT THE AUTHORS

Renod Bejjani is the cofounder of iHOPE Ministries and the primary architect of the ETHNOS Course. Raised as a Christian in several Islamic-ruled nations, Renod experienced intense persecution that left him wrestling with anger toward God and deep hostility toward Muslims. Through a profound work of grace, God transformed his heart—redirecting his life toward serving the very people he once feared and opposed.

Renod brings both theological depth and lived cross-cultural experience to his work. His passion is to help everyday believers confidently and compassionately share Jesus with people of other faiths—without fear, arguments, or expertise-driven approaches.

For more than a decade, Renod has trained churches, leaders, and ministry workers across cultures and continents. He is the author of *The Way to Paradise*, an evangelistic Bible study for Muslim seekers, and *Muslims: 5 Biblical Essentials Every Christian Must Know and Do*. His teaching emphasizes dependence on the Holy Spirit, faithfulness to Scripture, and simple obedience to Jesus that leads to lasting fruit.

ABOUT THE AUTHORS

Karen Bejjani is the cofounder of iHOPE Ministries and a primary architect of the ETHNOS Course. Growing up in America's heartland, Karen had little exposure to people of other faiths. She pursued the American Dream and built a successful corporate career, developing a gift for leadership, strategy, and coaching.

Today, Karen uses those same skills to embolden everyday Christians to live courageously for Christ across cultures. She is the creator of the Blue Cord Women's Initiative and the primary architect of The Blue Cord women's book study—resources designed to help women move from fear to faith-filled action in cross-faith relationships.

Through conferences, book studies, podcasts, and leadership pathways, Karen has helped thousands of women grow in confidence, compassion, and obedience. Her leadership blends biblical conviction, pastoral wisdom, and a deep belief that God delights in using ordinary believers to accomplish extraordinary kingdom work.

Together, Renod and Karen lead iHOPE Ministries with a shared vision: *to ignite and equip believers to boldly reveal Christ across faiths—so the world may know.*

www.ingramcontent.com/pod-product-compliance
Lightning Source LLC
Chambersburg PA
CBHW081430070526
44586CB00020B/2542